interchange

FOURTH EDITION

Jack C. Richards

With Jonathan Hull and Susan Proctor

Series Editor: David Bohlke

WORKBOOK 3

CAMBRIDGE
UNIVERSITY PRESS

CAMBRIDGE
UNIVERSITY PRESS

32 Avenue of the Americas, New York, NY 10013-2473, USA

Cambridge University Press is part of the University of Cambridge.

It furthers the University's mission by disseminating knowledge in the pursuit of education, learning and research at the highest international levels of excellence.

www.cambridge.org
Information on this title: www.cambridge.org/9781107648746

© Cambridge University Press 2013

This publication is in copyright. Subject to statutory exception and to the provisions of relevant collective licensing agreements, no reproduction of any part may take place without the written permission of Cambridge University Press.

First published 1995
Second edition 2000
Third edition 2005
14th printing 2015

Printed in Dubai by Oriental Press

A catalog record for this publication is available from the British Library.

ISBN 978-1-107-64870-8 Student's Book 3 with Self-study DVD-ROM
ISBN 978-1-107-69720-1 Student's Book 3A with Self-study DVD-ROM
ISBN 978-1-107-65269-9 Student's Book 3B with Self-study DVD-ROM
ISBN 978-1-107-64874-6 Workbook 3
ISBN 978-1-107-64685-8 Workbook 3A
ISBN 978-1-107-68752-3 Workbook 3B
ISBN 978-1-107-61506-9 Teacher's Edition 3 with Assessment Audio CD/CD-ROM
ISBN 978-1-107-66870-6 Class Audio 3 CDs
ISBN 978-1-107-66684-9 Full Contact 3 with Self-study DVD-ROM
ISBN 978-1-107-62042-1 Full Contact 3A with Self-study DVD-ROM
ISBN 978-1-107-63667-5 Full Contact 3B with Self-study DVD-ROM

For a full list of components, visit www.cambridge.org/interchange

Cambridge University Press has no responsibility for the persistence or accuracy of URLs for external or third-party Internet Web sites referred to in this publication and does not guarantee that any content on such Web sites is, or will remain, accurate or appropriate. Information regarding prices, travel timetables, and other factual information given in this work is correct at the time of first printing but Cambridge University Press does not guarantee the accuracy of such information thereafter.

Art direction, book design, layout services, and photo research: Integra

Contents

Credits

Illustrations

Andrezzinho: 23 (*bottom*), **Ilias Arahovitis**: 31, 69, 80; **Daniel Baxter**: 33, 96; **Mark Collins**: 4, 85; **Jeff Crosby**: 74 (*right and bottom*); **Carlos Diaz**: 53, 65, 66; **Jada Fitch**: 29; **Tim Foley**: 22, 26; **Travis Foster**: 14; **Dylan Gibson**: 84; **Chuck Gonzales**: 13 (*top*), 76, 77, 87; **Joaquin Gonzalez**: 16, 86; **Trevor Keen**: 6, 10

KJA-artists: 5, 20, 28, 90; **Greg Lawhun**: 18, 73; **Shelton Leong**: 1, 15 (*top right*), 25, 50, 64; **Karen Minot**: 19, 21, 32, 51; **Rob Schuster**: 11, 23 (*top*), 39, 88; **James Yamasaki**: 13 (*bottom*), 34, 78; **Rose Zgodzinski**: 15 (*magazine background*), 27, 45, 52, 57, 93; **Carol Zuber-Mallison**: 9, 17, 37, 63, 70, 75, 81

Photos

2 © Indeed/Getty Images
7 © Ton Koene/Picture Contact BV/Alamy
8 © AP Photo/Nick Wass
9 © Jason Kempin/Getty Images
12 (*clockwise from top left to right*) © Abdelhak Senna/AFP/Getty Images; © Jose Luis Pelaez Inc/Blend Images; © Getty Images/Creatas/Thinkstock; © Jose Luis Pelaez Inc/Blend Images/Getty Images;
17 © Jupiterimages/Brand X Pictures/Getty Images
19 (*top right*) © iStockphoto/Thinkstock; (*bottom right*) © AP Photo/Sakchai Lalit
24 (*top, left to right*) © Winston Davidian/Photodisc/Getty Images; © Dave & Les Jacobs/Blend Images/Alamy; © Yellow Dog Productions/The Image Bank/Getty Images; © Tetra Images/SuperStock; © Image Source/Getty Images
30 © AP Photo/Matt Sayles
32 (*top left*) © Jupiterimages/Comstock/Thinkstock; (*top right*) © Shioguchi/Taxi/Getty Images
37 (*top, left to right*) © Marvin Dembinsky Photo Associates/Alamy; © Garry D McMichael/Photo Researchers/Getty Images; © Stacy Gold/National Geographic/Getty Images; © Peter Donaldson/Alamy
38 © Thomas R. Fletcher/Alamy
40 © D. Hurst/Alamy
41 © Maisant Ludovic/hemis.fr/Getty Images
42 © A. Ramey/PhotoEdit
43 © Guido Vrola/iStockphoto
44 © age fotostock/SuperStock
45 © Stockbyte/Thinkstock
46 (*top, left to right*) © Asia Images Group/Getty Images; © Directphoto/age fotostock/SuperStock; © Andreea Manciu/The Agency Collection/Getty Images
47 (*top, left to right*) © Ghislain & Ma David de Lossy/The Image Bank/Getty Images; © Jupiterimages/Comstock/Thinkstock; © Redlink Production/Flame/Corbis; © Hill Street Studios/Blend Images/Getty Images
48 (*top right*) © Stephen Simpson/Taxi/Getty Images; (*middle right*) © Jon Feingersh/Blend Images/Getty Images
49 (*top to bottom*) © Eric Audras/Getty Images; © Jeff Morgan 10/Alamy; © Ron Levine/The Image Bank/Getty Images
52 © Image Source/Getty Images

54 © Mike Harrington/Digital Vision/Getty Images
55 (*middle right*) © Nick White/Digital Vision/Getty Images; (*bottom right*) © Jane Sweeney/The Image Bank/Getty Images
56 (*middle right*) © Simon Denyer/The Washington Post/Getty Images; (*bottom right*) © Hubertus Kanus/Photo Researchers/Getty Images
57 © Foto24/Gallo Images/Alamy
58 (*top left*) © Caspar Benson/fStop/Alamy; (*bottom right*) © Clerkenwell/The Agency Collection/Getty Images
59 © Justin Sullivan/Getty Images
60 © Javier Pierini/Taxi/Getty Images
61 © Leland Bobbe/Photographer's Choice/Getty Images
62 © Pascal Broze/Getty Images
63 © Michael Steele/Getty Images
67 © Nik Wheeler/Alamy
68 © Jeff Greenberg/PhotoEdit
70 © View Pictures Ltd/SuperStock
71 (*left to right*) © Used by permission of World Wildlife Fund and Ogilvy & Mather France; © Used by permission of Calgary Farmers' Market. Agency: WAX. Creative Directors: Joe Hospodarec, Monique Gamache. Art Director: Brian Allen. Copywriter: Stephanie Bialik, Photographer: Ken Woo Account Manager: Greg Thompson
74 © Peter Adams/Digital Vision/Getty Images
75 © Mira/Alamy
79 (*top left*) © Charlotte Wiig/Alamy; (*top right*) © Leonard Adam/Contributor/Getty Images
81 (*middle, left to right*) © Grant Faint/Photographer's Choice/Getty Images; © Zoonar/Thinkstock; © Milos Iuzanin/Alamy; © Nik Wheeler/Terra/Corbis
82 (*top left*) © Robert Nickelsberg/Contributor/Getty Images News/Getty Images; (*top right*) © Bonnie Jacobs/iStockphoto
83 © Bill Siel/Kenosha News
89 © Technotr/istockphoto
92 (*top left*) © Gaetano Images/Corbis Premium RF/Alamy; (*top right*) © DLILLC/Corbis RF/Alamy
93 © Ton Koene/Picture Contact BV/Alamy
94 (*top right*) © Javier Pierini/Photographer's Choice RF/Getty Images; (*bottom right*) © Courtesy of Peace Corps
95 © David Buffington/Blend Images/Getty Images

That's what friends are for!

1 Complete these descriptions with the words from the list.

1. John is so _____ modest _____ ! He always has such great ideas
   and never takes any credit for them.

2. The Chans like meeting new people and having friends over for dinner.
   They're one of the most _____ couples I know.

3. You can't trust Jane. She always promises to do something, but then
   she never does it. She's pretty _____ .

4. Alex wants to be an actor. It's hard to break into the business,
   but his family is very _____ of his dream.

5. I never know how to act around Tina! One minute she's in a good mood,
   and the next minute she's in a bad mood. She's *so* _____ .

✔	modest
☐	sociable
☐	supportive
☐	temperamental
☐	unreliable

2 Opposites

A Complete the chart by forming the opposites of the adjectives
in the list. Use *in-* and *un-*. Then check your answers in a dictionary.

✔ attractive	☐ dependent	☐ formal	☐ reliable
✔ competent	☐ experienced	☐ popular	☐ sensitive
☐ cooperative	☐ flexible	☐ reasonable	☐ sociable

incompetent

Opposites with *in-*		**Opposites with *un-***	
incompetent	_____	unattractive	_____
_____	_____	_____	_____
_____	_____	_____	_____

B Write four sentences using any of the words in part A.

Example: _Fred is very competent at work, but he's inexperienced. He still has a lot to learn._

1. _____

2. _____

3. _____

4. _____

1

3 Add *who* or *that* to the conversation where necessary.
Put an ✗ where *who* or *that* is not necessary.

A: I'm looking for someone _____✗_____ I can go on vacation with.

B: Hmm. So what kind of person are you looking for?

A: I want to travel with someone _____ is easygoing and independent.

B: Right. And you'd probably also like a person _____ is reliable.

A: Yeah, and I want someone _____ I know well.

B: So why don't you ask me?

A: You? I know you *too* well!

B: Ha! Does that mean you think I'm someone _____ is high-strung,
   dependent, and unreliable?

A: No! I'm just kidding. You're definitely someone _____ I could
   go on vacation with. So, . . . what are you doing in June?

4 Complete the sentences with *who* or *that* and your own information or ideas.

1. I generally like to go out with people <u>who are easygoing and have a sense of humor</u> .

2. I'd rather travel with someone _____ .

3. I don't really want a roommate _____ .

4. My classmates and I like teachers _____ .

5. My best friend and I want to meet people _____ .

6. Most workers would prefer a boss _____ .

7. Some people don't like stingy types _____ .

8. I don't want to have inflexible friends _____ .

9. I feel comfortable discussing my problems with friends _____ .

10. My favorite friends are people _____ .

5 Signs of fashion

A Scan the Chinese horoscope chart. Women of which two signs like jewelry?

Because Chinese New Year falls in January or February, the sign for someone born in either month could be the sign for the preceding year.

The Boar
1959 1971 1983 1995 2007 2019
Whether you are a man or a woman, you love dressing up. You are sociable, and you like to go to parties to show off your new clothes. If others don't notice them, you get upset.

The Rat
1960 1972 1984 1996 2008 2020
If you are a woman, you don't dress to impress people. But you like it when people notice your charm. If you are a man, you often wear what you threw on the floor the night before.

The Buffalo
1961 1973 1985 1997 2009 2021
You are a practical woman. You like to wear functional clothes during the day and dress much more colorfully at night. If you are a man, you are simply not interested in clothes.

The Dog
1958 1970 1982 1994 2006 2018
You like it when people like you. If you are a woman, you are neat and very stylish. If you are a man, you are no different.

The Tiger
1962 1974 1986 1998 2010 2022
You are the kind of woman who likes to wear strong colors or an unusual piece of jewelry. If you are a man, you like it when you dress differently from other men. When others have suits on, you'll wear jeans and a sweater.

The Rooster
1957 1969 1981 1993 2005 2017
Your hair is very important to you. Women who are born in these years always think first about their hair, and they don't care about their wardrobe. If you are a man, you are very similar.

The Monkey
1956 1968 1980 1992 2004 2016
If you are a woman, you have a large wardrobe, and you like to impress people with your choice of clothes. If you are a man, you don't worry too much about what you wear.

The Rabbit
1951 1963 1975 1987 1999 2011
Women usually have lovely hair and like beautiful things. They choose clothes carefully. Men are fussy about dressing and follow the latest trends.

The Goat
1955 1967 1979 1991 2003 2015
If you are a woman, you love to dress in style and with taste, and you have a very large closet. If you are a man, you really like to wear designer clothes.

The Horse
1954 1966 1978 1990 2002 2014
You like elegance, and you follow the latest fashions. If you are a woman, you know this already; however, if you are a man, it may take you a while to realize this.

The Snake
1953 1965 1977 1989 2001 2013
Women like to wear a lot of jewelry and other accessories. If you are a man, you think carefully about what you wear, and you have very good taste.

The Dragon
1952 1964 1976 1988 2000 2012
You are the kind of person who likes people to notice you, so you sometimes wear unusual clothes. Also, you often have trouble finding comfortable shoes, so you like to go barefoot.

B What do you think each person's sign is?

1. Steve's friends think he wears strange clothes. His favorite outfit is a bright red jacket with green pants and a purple tie.

   Sign: _____

2. Wanda loves to wear new clothes when she goes out. However, she gets really annoyed when people don't compliment her on what she's wearing.

   Sign: _____

3. Carl is the sort of man who doesn't pay much attention to his clothes, but his hair always looks great. He goes to the best salon in town.

   Sign: _____

4. Stephanie is someone who always wears extremely bright colors. She also usually wears an interesting necklace and earrings.

   Sign: _____

6 Match the clauses in column A with the most suitable clauses in column B.

A	B
1. I like it _____	a. when someone criticizes me in front of other people.
2. I don't mind it _____	b. when people are easygoing and friendly.
3. It upsets me _____	c. when rich people are stingy.
4. It embarrasses me _____	d. when people are a few minutes late for an appointment.

7 Write sentences about these situations. Use the expressions in the box.

I love it . . .	I can't stand it . . .	I don't like it . . .
It upsets me . . .	It bothers me . . .	I don't mind it . . .
I really like it . . .	It makes me happy . . .	It makes me angry . . .

1. <u>I don't like it when people cut in line.</u>
_____

2. _____
_____

3. _____
_____

4. _____
_____
_____

5. _____
_____
_____

6. _____
_____
_____

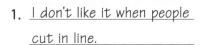

8 *What are some things you like and don't like about people? Write two sentences about each of the following. Use the ideas in the pictures and your own ideas.*

1. What I really like:

   I love it when someone is generous and

   gives me flowers.

   It makes me happy when

   _____

2. What I don't like:

   It bothers me when _____

   _____

   _____

3. What really doesn't bother me:

   I really don't mind it when _____

   _____

   _____

4. What upsets me:

   It upsets me when _____

   _____

   _____

9 It really bugs me!

Choose one thing from Exercise 8 that really embarrasses, bothers, or upsets you. Write two paragraphs about it. In the first paragraph, describe the situation. In the second paragraph, say why this situation is difficult for you and describe a situation you would prefer.

> It really embarrasses me when someone is too generous to me. Recently, I dated a guy who was always giving me things. For my birthday, he bought me an expensive necklace, and he treated me to dinner and a movie.
>
> The problem is, I don't have enough money to treat him in the same way. I'd prefer to date someone I have more in common with. In fact, my ideal boyfriend is someone who is sensible and saves his money!

_____

_____

_____

_____

_____

_____

_____

_____

10 Choose the correct word to complete each sentence.

1. I can tell Simon anything, and I know he won't tell anyone else.

   I can really _____ him. (believe / treat / trust)

2. Brenda has a very high opinion of herself. I don't like people who are

   so _____ . (egotistical / temperamental / supportive)

3. It bothers me when people are too serious. I prefer people who are

   _____ and have a good sense of humor. (easygoing / inflexible / reliable)

4. I like it when someone expresses strong _____ . Hearing other people's

   views can really make you think. (accomplishments / compliments / opinions)

5. Jackie is very rich, but she only spends her money on herself.

   She's very _____ . (generous / modest / stingy)

2 Career moves

1 What's your job?

A Match the jobs with their definitions.

A/An...   *is a person who....*

1. comedian __f__   a. researches environmentally friendly technologies

2. green researcher _____   b. helps students with their problems

3. guidance counselor _____   c. controls a company's brand online

4. organic food farmer _____   d. takes care of animals in captivity

5. social media manager _____   e. grows food without chemicals

6. zookeeper _____   f. makes people laugh for a living

B Write a definition for each of these jobs: accountant, fashion designer, and flight attendant.

1. An accountant is someone who _____

2. _____

3. _____

2 Challenging or frightening?

A Which words have a positive meaning, and which ones have a negative meaning? Write **P** or **N**.

awful __N__   fantastic _____

boring _____   fascinating _____

challenging _____   frightening _____

dangerous _____   interesting _____

difficult _____   rewarding _____

zookeeper

B Write about four jobs you know. Use the words in part A and gerund phrases.

Example: I think being a zookeeper would be fascinating.

1. _____

2. _____

3. _____

4. _____

3 Career choices

A Match each career and the most appropriate job responsibility.

Careers		Job responsibilities
work	for an airline	do research
	with computers	teach discipline and fitness
	as a high school coach	learn new software programs
be	a university professor	work independently
	a writer	travel to different countries

B Use the information from part A and gerund phrases to complete this conversation.

Ann: So, what kind of career would you like, Tom?

Tom: Well, I'm not exactly sure. _Being a writer_ could be interesting. Maybe blogging about something I'm interested in.

Ann: Hmm. I don't know if I'd like that because I'd have to write every day.

Tom: What do you want to do, then?

Ann: Well, I'm not sure either! I'd love _____ . I'd really enjoy being with teenagers all day and _____ . On the other hand, I'd be interested in _____ .

Tom: Really? What would you like about that?

Ann: Well, I'd love _____ all over the world.

Tom: Oh, I could never do that! I think it would be very tiring work.

C Write a short conversation like the one in part B. Use the remaining information in part A or your own ideas.

A: So, what kind of career would you like?

B: Well, I'm not exactly sure. _____

A: That sounds interesting. But I wouldn't like it because _____

B: What do you want to do, then?

A: Well, I'd love _____

B: _____

A: _____

4 *What a job!*

A Read the magazine interviews. Write the correct job title above each interview.

☐ aerobics instructor   ☐ freelance artist   ☐ house painter   ☐ orchestra conductor
☐ child-care worker   ☐ graphic designer   ☐ musician   ☐ self-employed builder

Tell us about your job

1 _____

All my friends seem to earn more than I do. I suppose it's easier if you have a 9 to 5 job. I work on people's houses and manage construction sites all day. I stay pretty fit doing that, and I enjoy being outside. But in the evenings, I have to make phone calls and do paperwork. It never seems to end!

2 _____

Working for yourself is hard because you are responsible for everything. If no one calls you and asks you to work for them, you have to go out and look for work. Luckily, I now have some regular clients. I paint pictures for some expensive hotels. Right now, I'm doing some paintings for the rooms of a new hotel in Hawaii.

3 _____

My friends say my work is less demanding than theirs, but I work just as hard as they do. I spend a lot of time alone because my job can't begin until all the construction work is completed. Usually, the rooms look great when I've finished my work. Sometimes customers choose really ugly colors, but I have to do what they want.

4 _____

The musicians I lead are extremely talented, and we work together to make sure they sound as good as possible. We often work evenings and weekends, and we travel a lot. Working with a large number of people can be challenging, and it really bothers me if someone is moody because it affects everyone else.

orchestra conductor

5 _____

Keeping fit is really important to me. What could be better than doing a job that makes you really fit? Of course, a lot of my students are very unfit — that's why they come to my classes! But that's also why I love my work. After several weeks, most of my students look and feel much better than they did on the first day of class.

6 _____

Being with kids all day isn't for everyone, but I love it. I take care of the children when their parents are away. I do all kinds of things – I teach, I play games, and I read books. I make sure the children are safe and happy. I have a lot of responsibility, but I love my job. The pay isn't great, but it's very rewarding work.

B Underline the words and phrases that helped you find the answers in part A.

5 First, use words from the list to complete the name of each job title. Then choose the best expressions to compare the jobs in each sentence.

▢ assistant ▢ decorator ▢ painter ▢ walker
▢ counselor ▢ instructor ▢ ranger ☑ worker

1. A child-care _____worker_____ doesn't earn _____as much as_____ an accountant.
   ☑ as much as ▢ greater than ▢ worse than

2. A chef's _____ has _____ a waiter.
   ▢ as bad hours as ▢ not as good hours as ▢ worse hours than

3. A dog _____ is _____ a student intern.
   ▢ more interesting than ▢ not as boring as ▢ better paid than

4. A house _____ earns _____ a camp counselor.
   ▢ as bad as ▢ more than ▢ not more than

5. A park _____ is _____ a landscaper.
   ▢ as bad as ▢ not as well paid as ▢ worse than

6. Being a yoga _____ is _____ being a professor.
   ▢ more than ▢ as much as ▢ not as difficult as

7. Being an interior _____ is _____ being a sales assistant.
   ▢ greater than ▢ earns more than ▢ more interesting than

8. A guidance _____ has _____ a gardener.
   ▢ more responsibility than ▢ not more than ▢ not as long as

6 Complete these sentences with the correct prepositions. Some of the prepositions may be used more than once. More than one answer may be possible.

1. Wai-man works _____ the best Chinese restaurant in Vancouver.

2. I think working _____ other people is more fun than working alone.

3. I would hate working _____ the media. It would be nerve-racking!

4. Working _____ a dance instructor sounds great.

5. Working _____ an office is less interesting than working _____ a cruise ship.

▢ as
▢ at
▢ in
▢ on
▢ with

7 *Use the words in parentheses to compare the jobs.*

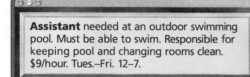

Assistant needed at an outdoor swimming pool. Must be able to swim. Responsible for keeping pool and changing rooms clean. $9/hour. Tues.–Fri. 12–7.

Learn web design! In search of a bright young person to work as an intern for an advertising agency. Some clerical work. $10/hour. Mon.–Fri. 9–5.

1. A: <u>An assistant at a swimming pool has shorter hours than an intern.</u>
   (shorter hours)

   B: <u>Yes, but working as an intern is more interesting than being a swimming pool assistant.</u>
   (interesting)

Travel agency needs energetic people. Knowledge of a second language is a plus. Mostly answering the phone. $12/hour. Flexible hours. Three vacation days.

Tutors in math, science, English, and music wanted at private summer school. Challenging work with gifted teenagers. Salary negotiable. Mon.–Sat. 3–7.

2. A: <u>Working in a</u>
   (better benefits)

   B: <u>Yes, but working</u>
   (challenging)

Tennis instructor needed at summer camp for 12- and 13-year-olds. Must be excellent tennis player and good with kids. $12/hour. Mon.–Fri. 1–7.

Tour company seeks **guide** to lead bus tours. Great attitude and good speaking voice a must! Fun work, but must be willing to work long hours. $15/hour.

3. A: _____
   (make as much money)

   B: _____
   (work longer hours)

City seeks **taxi drivers** for morning shift. No experience necessary; driver's license required. $10/hour plus tips. Mon.–Thu. 7 A.M.–2 P.M.

Office assistant required in small, friendly office. Computer skills an advantage. Interesting work. Some management skills necessary. $15/hour. 6-day week.

4. A: _____
   (a shorter work week)

   B: _____
   (less boring)

8 *Choose four pairs of jobs from the box below to compare.*
Say which job you would prefer and give two reasons.

- a graphic designer/a TV news director
- an architect/a teacher
- a guidance counselor/a coach
- a doctor/a musician

- a police officer/a politician
- a secret agent/a psychiatrist
- working on a construction site/ working in an office
- being self-employed/working for a company

Example: Working as a TV news director sounds more interesting than being a graphic designer. A TV news director has more responsibility than a graphic designer. Also, directing the news is better paid.

1. _____

_____

_____

2. _____

_____

_____

3. _____

_____

_____

4. _____

_____

_____

3 Could you do me a favor?

 Would you mind . . . ?

A Complete the request for each situation.

1. You want to borrow a dollar from a friend for a cup of coffee.

   Can I borrow a dollar for a cup of coffee?

2. You want a classmate to give you a ride home after class.

   Would you mind

3. You want to turn down your roommate's TV.

   Is it OK if

4. You want to use a friend's cell phone.

   Do you mind if

5. You want to borrow a friend's car for the weekend.

   I was wondering if

6. You want someone to tell you how to get to the subway.

   Could

B Think of four things you would need to have done if you were going on a long vacation. Write requests asking a friend to do the things.

Example: *Could you water the plants?*

1. _____

2. _____

3. _____

4. _____

2 *Accept or decline these requests. For requests you decline, give excuses.*
Use the expressions in the box or expressions of your own.

Accepting	Declining
That's OK, I guess.	Sorry, but . . .
I'd be glad to.	I'd like to, but . . .
Fine. No problem.	Unfortunately, . . .

1. A: Can I use your computer? My computer crashed.

   B: <u>Sorry, but I'm going to use it myself in</u>
   <u>a few minutes.</u>

2. A: I've just finished this ten-page paper. Could you check it for me, please?

   B: _____

3. A: I was wondering if I could stay at your place for a week while my landlord fixes the roof.

   B: _____

4. A: Would you mind if I used your cell phone to make a long-distance call to Nigeria?

   B: _____

3 *Look at the pictures and write the conversations. Speaker A makes a request.*
Speaker B declines it. Each speaker should give a reason.

1. A: <u>Could you carry these suitcases</u>
   <u>for me? I have a bad back.</u>

   B: <u>Sorry, but I have a bad back, too.</u>

2. A: _____

   _____

   B: _____

   _____

3. A: _____

   _____

   B: _____

   _____

A Scan the magazine article about making requests. When do people often make formal requests? When do they make less formal requests?

Requests that get RESULTS

> DO YOU HAVE **TWO THOUSAND DOLLARS** FOR A CUP OF COFFEE? I WANT TO DRINK IT IN **BRAZIL!**

There are many different ways of making requests. For example, if someone wants to borrow a dollar, he or she can say:

"Could you lend me a dollar?"
"Do you have a dollar?"
"You don't have a dollar, do you?"

How does a person know which request to use? Language researchers have suggested that speakers must make several important decisions. First, they must consider the other person's feelings because requests can sometimes cause embarrassment to both the speaker and the listener. If the speaker thinks the listener will accept the request, he or she will probably use a less formal request; however, if the speaker thinks the listener may decline the request, he or she will probably use a fairly formal request. The listener then has to make a choice either to accept or refuse the request. If he or she refuses, then both the speaker and the listener might be embarrassed.

In addition, speakers must decide how well they know the person they are requesting something from and choose a suitable question. If the speaker knows the listener well, one of several types of requests can be used. For example:

1. **Make a statement with *need*:** "I need a dollar."
2. **Use an imperative:** "Please lend me a dollar."
3. **Use a question:** "Do you have a dollar?"

If the speaker doesn't know the listener well, one of several types of requests can be used instead. For example:

4. **Ask about ability:** "Could/Can you lend me a dollar?"
5. **Be polite – use *may*:** "May I borrow a dollar?"
6. **Ask for permission:** "Would it be OK if I borrowed a dollar?"
7. **Express curiosity:** "I wonder if I could borrow a dollar."
8. **State the request negatively:** "I don't suppose you could lend me a dollar."
9. **Apologize:** "I hope you don't mind my asking, but could I borrow a dollar?"
10. **Give a hint:** "I don't have any cash on me."

Knowing how to make requests means knowing different types of requests as well as when each type of request is appropriate.

B Read the article. Check (✓) if each request is less formal or more formal. Then write the correct number from the article (1–10) for each type of request.

	Less formal	More formal	Type
1. Close the door.	☐	☐	____
2. It's really cold in here.	☐	☐	____
3. Could you possibly move your car?	☐	☐	____
4. May I borrow your dictionary?	☐	☐	____
5. I was wondering if you could help me with this assignment.	☐	☐	____
6. I need some help moving to my new apartment.	☐	☐	____
7. I'm sorry, but I can't stand loud music.	☐	☐	____
8. Do you have a camera?	☐	☐	____

5 Nouns and verbs

A Complete this chart. Then check your answers in a dictionary.

Noun	Verb	Noun	Verb
apology	_apologize_	invitation	_____
compliment	_____	permission	_____
explanation	_____	request	_____

B Check (✓) the phrase that describes what each person is doing.

I really like your new haircut.

1. I really like your new haircut.
   ☐ giving a reason
   ☐ giving a compliment

2. Don't worry. I know you didn't mean to break it.
   ☐ returning a favor
   ☐ accepting an apology

3. Can I borrow your laptop?
   ☐ asking for a favor
   ☐ giving a gift

4. I can't lend you my bike because I need it myself.
   ☐ declining a request
   ☐ accepting an invitation

5. Could you help me cook dinner?
   ☐ making a request
   ☐ returning a compliment

6 Choose the correct words.

1. My phone didn't work for a week. The phone company

   _____ an apology and took $20 off my bill.

   (accepted / denied / offered)

2. A friend of mine really loves to _____ compliments, but

   he never gives anyone else one. I don't understand why he's like that.

   (do / owe / receive)

3. Carol is always talking on the phone. She makes a lot of calls, but she rarely

   _____ mine. Maybe she never listens to her voice mail!

   (makes / offers / returns)

4. I need to _____ a favor. Could you please give

   me a ride to school tomorrow? My bike has a flat tire!

   (ask for / give / turn down)

7 *Use these messages to complete the phone conversations.*
Use indirect requests.

1 Message
For: Rosa,
Ms. Anita Jensen called.
Her flight arrives at 7 p.m.
on Tuesday. Please meet
her in the International
Arrivals area.

2 Message
For: Eric,
Kevin called this morning.
Can he borrow your
scanner? If yes, when
can he pick it up?

3 Message
For: Alex,
Mr. Todd called yesterday.
The meeting is on Thursday
at 10:30 a.m. Don't forget to
bring your report.

4 Message
For: Jenny,
Philip Lim called earlier. Are
you going to the conference
tomorrow? What time does
it start?

1. A: Is Rosa Sanchez there, please?

   B: No, she isn't. Would you like to leave a message?

   A: Yes, please. This is Anita Jensen calling from Toronto.

   Could you tell her <u>that my flight arrives at 7 p.m. on Tuesday</u>   ?

   Would _____ ?

   B: OK, I'll give her the message.

2. A: Can I speak to Eric, please?

   B: I'm afraid he's not here. Do you want to leave a message?

   A: Yes, please. This is Kevin. Please _____ .

   And if it's OK, could you _____ ?

   B: Sure, I'll leave him the message.

3. A: Could I speak to Alex, please?

   B: I'm sorry, but he's not here right now.

   A: Oh, OK. This is Mr. Todd. I'd like to leave a message.

   Could _____ ?

   Could _____ ?

4. A: I'd like to speak to Jenny, please.

   B: She's not here right now. Can I take a message?

   A: Yeah. This is Philip Lim.

   Can _____ ?

   And would _____ ?

   B: OK, I'll give Jenny your message.

8 *Complete the conversation with the information in the box. Add any words necessary and use the correct form of the verbs given.*

☐ ask Jill to get some soda   ☐ bring a big salad
☐ borrow some money   ☐ buy dessert
☑ borrow your stereo   ☐ don't be late

Chris: So, is there anything I can do to help for the party?

Len: Yeah. Would it be all right _if I borrowed your stereo_ ?
Mine isn't working very well.

Chris: Sure. And I'll bring two extra speakers. We'll have amazing sound.

Len: Thanks.

Chris: No problem. Now, what about food?

Len: Well, I thought maybe a salad. Would you mind
_____ , too?

Chris: Well, OK. And how about drinks?

Len: Well, could you _____?
And please tell her _____ .
Last time we had a party, she didn't arrive till eleven o'clock,
and everyone got really thirsty!

Chris: I remember.

Len: One more thing – I was wondering if you could _____ .

Chris: Um, sure. All right. But, uh, would you mind if I
_____ to pay for it?

---

9 *Rewrite these sentences. Find another way to say each sentence using the words given.*

1. Can I use your cell phone?
   Would it be OK if I used your cell phone? _____ (OK)

2. Please ask Penny to stop by and talk to me.
   _____ (would)

3. Could I borrow your guitar?
   _____ (wonder)

4. Would you ask Adam what time he's coming over?
   _____ (could / when)

5. Lend me your hairbrush.
   _____ (mind)

What a story!

1 **Complete these news stories using the verbs from the list.**

☐ broke   ☐ found   ☐ locking   ☐ stayed   ☑ went
☐ drank   ☐ heard   ☐ shouted   ☐ waiting   ☐ wondered

1.

Woman trapped in bathroom for 20 days

A 69-year-old grandmother in Paris _____went_____ to the bathroom –

and _____ there for twenty days. What happened? As she

was _____ the door, the lock _____.

She could not open the door. She _____ for help, but

no one _____ her because her bathroom had no windows.

After nearly three weeks, the woman's neighbors _____ where she was. Firefighters

broke into her apartment and _____ her in a "very weakened" state. While she was

_____ to be rescued, she _____ warm water.

☐ became   ☐ checking in   ☐ entered   ☐ opened   ☐ sleeping
☐ behaving   ☐ decided   ☐ had   ☐ showed

2.

TIGER CUB FOUND IN LUGGAGE

A woman was _____ strangely when she _____

Bangkok airport. While she was _____ for an overseas flight, she

_____ difficulty with a very large bag. The check-in clerk

_____ suspicious and _____ to X-ray the bag.

The X-ray _____ an image that looked like an animal. When airport

staff _____ the bag, they saw that a baby tiger was

_____ under lots of toy tigers. The tiger was taken to a rescue

center for wildlife, and the woman was arrested.

2 Join each sentence in column A with an appropriate sentence in column B. Use *as*, *when*, or *while* to join the sentences.

A	B
I was crossing the road.	My racquet broke.
I was using my computer.	A car nearly hit me.
We were playing tennis.	The water got cold.
I was taking a shower.	I burned my finger.
I was cooking dinner.	It suddenly stopped working.

1. As I was crossing the road, a car nearly hit me.

2. _____

3. _____

4. _____

5. _____

3 Complete these conversations. Use the past tense or the past continuous of the verbs given.

1. A: Guess what happened to me last night! As
      I ___was getting___ (get) into bed, I _____ (hear)
      a loud noise like a gunshot in the street. Then the
      phone _____ (ring).

   B: Who was it?

   A: It was Mariana. She always calls me late at night,
      but this time she had a reason. She _____ (drive)
      right past my apartment when she _____ (get)
      a flat tire. It was very late, so while we _____
      (change) the tire, I _____ (invite) her to spend
      the night.

2. A: I'm sorry I'm so late, Kathy. I was at the dentist.

   B: Don't tell me! While you _____ (sit) in the waiting
      room, you _____ (meet) someone interesting.
      I know how you are, Tom!

   A: Well, you're wrong this time. The dentist _____
      (clean) my teeth when she suddenly _____ (get)
      called away for an emergency. So I just sat there waiting
      for two hours with my mouth hanging open!

4 *Lost and found*

A Read this news story. Check (✓) the best title.

☐ Phone call wakes man in hotel ☐ Small boat sails from Indonesia to Australia
☐ Text message saves 18 people ☐ Coast guards unable to rescue passengers

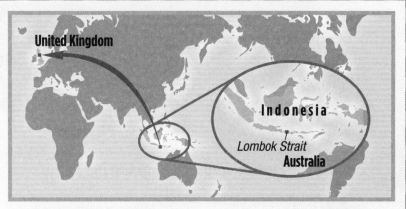

𝒜 boat with eighteen people on board – twelve tourists from the U.K., Australia, and New Zealand, and six Indonesian crew members – got into trouble somewhere between the islands of Bali and Lombok in Indonesia. Waves nearly five meters high struck the 23-meter boat. The engine broke down, and there was only a small generator that provided power for three lights on board. The boat had no marine radio.

Luckily, however, one of the tourists, a teenager named Rebecca Fyfe, had a cell phone. She sent a text message to her boyfriend, Nick Hodgson, who was asleep in a hotel in the U.K. The message woke him, and he immediately called her. They couldn't talk for long because her

battery was low, and she couldn't give the boat's exact position in the Lombok Straits. Nick then called a branch of the British coast guard, who contacted coast guards in both Indonesia and Australia.

Although the coast guards were unable to contact Rebecca because her cell phone battery

was now dead, an Indonesian navy boat and another ship soon found them. They were unable to rescue them immediately because the waves were still too high. Eventually, the boat and everyone on board arrived safely in a small port in the Gili Islands, about 100 kilometers east of Bali.

B Answer these questions.

1. Who was on the boat?

_____

2. Why did the boat get into trouble? (Give more than one reason.)

_____

3. Why did Rebecca Fyfe text her boyfriend?

_____

4. What did her boyfriend do after he received the text message?

_____

5. What stopped the coast guards from rescuing the passengers and crew quickly?

_____

6. How do you think the small boat arrived safely in the Gili Islands?

_____

5 *Imagine you had a problem like the people on the boat in Exercise 4.*
Write two paragraphs. In the first paragraph, describe the problem.
In the second, say how you solved it.

_____

_____

_____

_____

_____

_____

_____

_____

> A couple of years ago, I got lost
> in the mountains. I was hiking when
> it suddenly got foggy. I was really
> frightened because I couldn't see
> anything, and it was getting cold.
> I decided to put up my tent and
> stay there for the night.
>   While I was putting up my tent,
> though, the fog began to clear. . . .

6 *Choose the correct verbs to complete the story.*

Grammar note: After

In sentences using **after** *that show one past event occurring before another, the clause with* **after** *usually uses the past perfect.*

After she **had called** her friend, her cell phone battery died.

Bob and I ___had just gotten___ engaged, so we
            (just got / had just gotten)

went to a jewelry store to buy a wedding ring. We _____ a ring when a
                                                    (just chose / had just chosen)

masked man _____ . After the robber _____ Bob's
           (came in / had come in)   (took / had taken)

wallet, he _____ the ring. I _____ it to him when the
           (demanded / had demanded)   (just handed / had just handed)

alarm _____ to go off, and the robber _____ . We were
      (started / had started)   (ran off / had run off)

so relieved! But then the sales assistant _____ us we had to pay for the ring
                                          (told / had told)

because I _____ it to the robber. We _____ her
          (gave / had given)   (just told / had just told)

that we wouldn't pay for it when the police _____ and
                                            (arrived / had arrived)

_____ us! What a terrible experience!
(arrested / had arrested)

7 *What a story!*

A Choose the best headline for each of these news stories.

> **What a disaster!**
> **What a lucky break!**
> **What a triumph!**
> **What an emergency!**
> **What a dilemma!**

1. _____
Joan Smith was seven months pregnant when she and her husband, Hank, went on vacation to a small **remote** island off the coast of South America. On the first night, Joan was in a lot of pain. There were no doctors on the island, so Hank called a hospital on the **mainland**. They told him they could not send a helicopter because a typhoon was coming. During the night, Joan thought she was going to die. Luckily, the typhoon had passed over the island by the following morning. A helicopter picked Joan up and took her to the hospital – just in time for her to have a beautiful baby girl.

2. _____
Victoria Peters was very sick for several months before her final exams this summer. She couldn't study at all. Her parents suggested she should **skip** a year and take the exams the next summer. **Remarkably**, Victoria suddenly got well just before the exams, spent the next two weeks studying, and got the highest grade in her class!

3. _____
Jesse Peterson had waited years for a **promotion**. Finally, a week ago, he was offered the position he had always wanted – Regional Manager. On the same day, however, he won $6 million in the lottery. Jesse's wife wants him to **resign** from his job and take her on a trip around the world. Jesse says he cannot decide what to do.

B Look at the words in **bold** in the article. What do you think they mean?

remote _____   skip _____   promotion _____

mainland _____   remarkably _____   resign _____

8 *Complete the sentences. Use the simple past, the past continuous, or the past perfect of the verbs given.*

1. After an art show ___opened___ (open) in New York, it was discovered that someone _____ (hang) a famous painting by Henri Matisse upside down.

2. In 2003, Italian workers _____ (find) important archaeological remains while they _____ (construct) a new parking lot in Vatican City. There were mosaics dating from 54 to 68 CE.

3. Russia _____ (have) a very hot summer in 2010. The country _____ (not experience) such hot weather for at least 130 years.

4. In 2011, two divers _____ (discover) the remains of a 200-year-old shipwreck while they _____ (dive) off the coast of Rhode Island, in the eastern United States.

9 *Read this situation. Then use the information and clues to complete the chart. Write the name of each reporter and each country. (You will leave one square in the chart blank.)*

Ms. Anderson

Ms. Benson

Mr. Jackson

Mr. Marks

Mr. Swire

Five news reporters – two women and three men – arrived for an international conference on Sunday, Monday, and Tuesday. No more than two people came on the same day. The reporters came from five different countries.

Clues

The women:	Ms. Anderson and Ms. Benson
The men:	Mr. Jackson, Mr. Marks, and Mr. Swire
The countries:	Australia, Canada, Italy, Singapore, and the United States

The arrivals:

• Mr. Swire arrived late at night. No one else had arrived that day.

• Ms. Anderson and Mr. Marks arrived on the same day.

  The man from Singapore had arrived the day before.

• The reporters from Italy and Australia arrived on the same day.

• Mr. Jackson and the woman from Italy arrived on Tuesday, after Mr. Marks.

• The reporter from Australia arrived the day after the person from the United States.

• Mr. Marks is from North America but not the United States.

Reporters' countries and arrival days		
Sunday	Name: _____ Country: _____	Name: _____ Country: _____
Monday	Name: _____ Country: _____	Name: _____ Country: _____
Tuesday	Name: _____ Country: _____	Name: _____ Country: _____

5 Crossing cultures

1 *Complete these sentences. Use words from the list.*

- ☐ confident
- ☐ curious
- ☐ depressed
- ☑ embarrassed
- ☐ fascinated
- ☐ uncertain
- ☐ uncomfortable
- ☐ worried

1. In my country, people never leave tips. So when I first went abroad, I kept forgetting to tip servers. I felt really ___embarrassed___ .

2. The first time I traveled abroad, I felt really _____ . I was alone, I didn't speak the language, and I didn't make any friends.

3. I just spent a year in France learning to speak French. It was a satisfying experience, and I was _____ by the culture.

4. At first I really didn't like shopping in the open-air markets. I felt _____ because so many people were trying to sell me something at the same time.

5. When I arrived in Lisbon, I was nervous because I couldn't speak any Portuguese. As I began to learn the language, though, I became more _____ about living there.

6. Before I went to Alaska last winter, I was very _____ about the cold. But it wasn't a problem because most buildings there are well heated.

7. When I was traveling in Southeast Asia, I couldn't believe how many different kinds of fruit there were. I was _____ to try all of them, so I ate a lot of fruit!

8. It was our first trip to Latin America, so we were _____ about what to expect. We loved it and hope to return again soon.

2 *Imagine you are going to travel to a country you have never visited before. Write sentences using the factors and feelings given. Then add another sentence explaining your feelings.*

Factors	Feelings
public transportation	anxious (about)
the architecture	comfortable (with)
the climate	curious (about)
the food	enthusiastic (about)
the language	fascinated (by)
the money	nervous (about)
the music	uncertain (about)
the people my age	uncomfortable (with)

Example:

Public transportation is something I'd be anxious about.

I'd be afraid of getting lost.

1. _____

_____

2. _____

_____

3. _____

_____

4. _____

_____

5. _____

_____

6. _____

_____

7. _____

_____

8. _____

_____

3 *Culture shock!*

A Make a list of four pieces of advice to help people feel comfortable about traveling abroad.

B Scan the article about cultural differences. Where can you find articles like this? Who was it written for?

Each society has its own beliefs, attitudes, customs, behaviors, and social habits. These things give people a sense of who they are and how they are supposed to behave.

People become conscious of such rules when they meet people from different cultures. For example, the rules about when to eat vary from culture to culture. Many North Americans and Europeans organize their timetables around three mealtimes a day. In other countries, however, it's not the custom to have strict rules like this – people eat when they want to, and every family has its own timetable.

When people visit or live in a country for the first time, they are often surprised at the differences between this culture and the culture in their own country. For some people, traveling abroad is the thing they enjoy most in life; for others, cultural differences make them feel uncomfortable, frightened, and insecure. This is known as "culture shock."

When you're visiting a foreign country, it is important to understand and appreciate cultural differences. This can help you avoid misunderstandings, develop friendships more easily, and feel more comfortable when traveling or living abroad.

Here are several things to do in order to avoid culture shock.

1. Avoid quick judgments; try to understand the point of view of the people in another culture.

2. Become aware of what is going on around you, and why.

3. Don't think of your cultural habits as "right" and other people's as "wrong."

4. Be willing to try new things and to have new experiences.

5. Try to understand and appreciate other people's values.

6. Think about your own culture and how it influences your attitudes and actions.

7. Avoid having negative stereotypes about foreigners and their cultures.

8. Show interest in things that are important to other people.

C Read the article. Use your own words to write definitions for these words.

1. culture _____

2. culture shock _____

3. appreciate _____

4. stereotypes _____

D After reading the article, would you make any changes to the pieces of advice you listed in part A?

4 *Complete these sentences by giving information about customs in a country you know.*

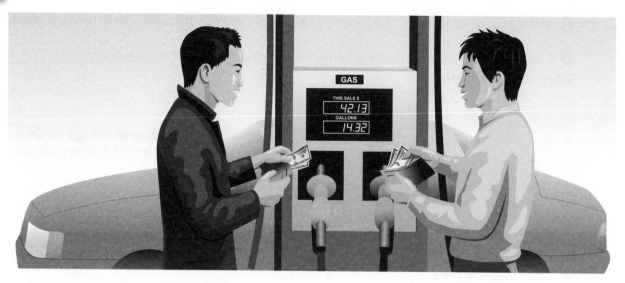

1. If you go for a long ride in a friend's car,

   <u>it's the custom to offer to pay for some of the expenses.</u>

2. When a friend graduates from school or college, _____

   _____

3. If you borrow something from a friend, _____

   _____

4. When a friend invites you to dinner, _____

   _____

5 *Contrasting customs*

A Read the information about the different customs and find four pairs of countries with contrasting customs. Write the countries in the blanks below.

Country	Custom
Brazil	Friends kiss each other three or four times on the cheeks as a greeting.
Denmark	People generally arrive on time for most occasions.
Egypt	People allow their hosts to treat them to meals in restaurants.
France	Service is usually included in the price of a meal in restaurants.
Japan	People bow when they see or meet someone they know.
New Zealand	People usually pay for their own meals in restaurants.
Spain	People usually arrive late for most appointments.
United States	People leave a tip of 15–20 percent in restaurants.

1. <u>Brazil and Japan</u>   3. _____

2. _____   4. _____

B Read these five cross-cultural situations. Write sentences describing what the visitors did wrong. Use the expressions in the box.

you're (not) supposed to
you're (not) expected to
it's (not) the custom to
it's (not) acceptable to

1. Hanne is from Denmark. When she was on vacation in Spain, some Spanish friends invited her to dinner at 9:00. She arrived at exactly 9:00, but her friends had not even arrived home yet.

   In Spain, you're expected to _____

   _____

2. Marylou is from the United States. During her first week in Paris, she went to a restaurant with some new friends. She was so happy with the service that she left a tip of 20 percent. Her friends were a little embarrassed.

   In France, _____

   _____

3. Peter is from New Zealand. When he went to Egypt, he was invited to dinner at a restaurant. When the bill came, he offered to pay for his dinner. His Egyptian friend was kind of upset.

   In Egypt, _____

   _____

4. Susana is from Brazil. She was working for a year in Osaka, Japan. One day, when she saw a Japanese co-worker in a bookstore, she went to say hello and kissed him on the cheeks. Her friend was very surprised.

   _____

   _____

5. Adam is from Canada. He was on vacation in Bali, Indonesia, and some new friends invited him to a temple to watch a special dance performance. He arrived on time wearing a clean T-shirt and shorts, but they said he couldn't go inside the temple because he wasn't dressed properly.

   _____

   _____

6 Complete these sentences with information about yourself (1–4) and about a country you know well (5–8).

1. One reason I'd feel homesick abroad is _____

2. Something that would fascinate me would be _____

3. Traveling alone is something _____

4. Getting used to hot weather is one thing _____

5. In _____ , it's the custom to _____

6. If you have good service in a restaurant, _____

7. You're expected to _____ when _____

8. It's just not acceptable to _____ if _____

7 Write about living in a foreign country. In the first paragraph, write about two things you would enjoy. In the second paragraph, write about two things you might worry about.

> If I lived in Colombia, I'd enjoy learning about the music scene – the local bands and singers who are popular there. Another thing I'd be fascinated by is . . .
>
> However, one thing that I'd be nervous about is the food. It might be very different from what I know. Something else I might be uncomfortable with is . . .

_____

_____

_____

_____

_____

_____

_____

_____

_____

_____

_____

What's wrong with it?

1 Can we fix it?

A What can be wrong with these things? Put these words in the correct categories.
(Most words go in more than one category.)

| bike | blouse | car | carpet | chair | glasses | plate | sink | tablecloth |

chipped	cracked	dented	leaking	scratched	stained	torn

B What is wrong with these things? Use the words in part A to write a sentence
about each one.

1. _The car is scratched._ OR
There's a scratch on the car.

2. _____

3. _____

4. _____

5. _____

6. _____

7. _____

8. _____

9. _____

2 *Problems, problems, problems!*

A Scan the articles in *Consumer* magazine. Who would read articles like these? Why?

Consumer

Sharon's laptops

Sharon Kurtz is a freelance writer who works at home. She bought a laptop from Star Superstore, a discount computer center. When she took it home, she discovered that the screen was fuzzy. The store agreed to exchange it. When a new laptop was delivered to her home, Sharon found that the outside cover was scratched. Again she complained, so the store offered her a third computer, but this one didn't work right either. Some of the keys on the keyboard were loose. She was offered a fourth laptop, but it crashed a week after she started using it.

At this point, Sharon got angry and contacted *Consumer* magazine. We wrote Star Superstore a letter explaining that Sharon was losing work because of all the computer problems. The store offered Sharon a full refund plus $1,000 for all the inconvenience she had suffered.

Chris's car

Chris Hill thought his troubles were over when the police found his stolen car, but in fact, his problems were only just beginning. The engine was badly damaged, and it needed to be replaced at a cost of $3,300. In addition, the locks were broken, and they needed to be repaired at a cost of $600. Chris's insurance company told him that he would have to pay 40 percent of the cost of the new engine ($1,320). They argued that the new engine would add 40 percent to the value of his car. However, Chris did not believe this.

Chris knew that the value of a used car depends mainly on its age, so he contacted *Consumer* magazine. One of our lawyers asked the insurance company to prove that the new engine would increase the value of the car. When the insurance company replied, they said they no longer wanted Chris to pay any of the repair costs.

B Read the article and complete the chart. Did Sharon and Chris receive money?

	Problems	What *Consumer* magazine did	Paid back?	
			Yes	No
1. Sharon's laptops	fuzzy screen		☐	☐
2. Chris's car			☐	☐

3 *Choose appropriate verbs to complete the sentences. Use passive infinitives (to be + past participle) or gerunds.*

> ### Language note: Verbs ending in -en or -n
>
> **Some verbs are formed by adding -en or -n to a noun or adjective. These verbs mean "to make more of something."**
>
> | Noun | | Verb | Adjective | | Verb |
> |------|---|------|-----------|---|------|
> | length | → | length**en** | loose | → | loos**en** |
> | (make something longer) | | | (make something looser) | | |

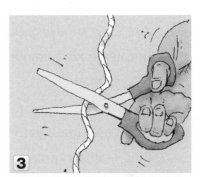

☑ lengthen   ☐ loosen   ☐ sharpen   ☐ shorten   ☐ tighten   ☐ widen

1. This jacket is too short.

   <u>It needs to be lengthened.</u>   OR

   <u>It needs lengthening.</u>

2. The screws on these glasses are too loose.

   They need _____

3. The blades on these scissors are too dull.

   They need _____

4. This faucet is too tight.

   It needs _____

5. These pants are too long.

   They need _____

6. This street is too narrow.

   It needs _____

4 *Complete the conversation. Use* keep, keeps, need, *or* needs
with passive infinitives or gerunds of the verbs given.

Tim: Guess what? Someone broke into my car last night!

Jan: Oh, no. What did they take?

Tim: Nothing! But they did a lot of damage. The lock <u>needs to be repaired</u> . (repair)

And the window _____ . (replace)

Jan: It was probably some young kids having "fun."

Tim: Yeah, some fun. I think they had a party in my car!

The seats _____ . (clean)

Jan: How annoying. Does the car drive OK?

Tim: No, it feels strange. The gears _____ (stick),

so they _____ . (fix) And the

brakes _____ (check) right away.

Jan: Well, I guess you're lucky they didn't steal it!

Tim: Yeah, lucky me.

5 *Write about something you bought that had something wrong with it.
In the first paragraph, describe the problem. In the second paragraph,
explain what you did about it.*

> Recently, I bought an espresso machine. While I was unpacking it,
> I could see it was already damaged. The glass carafe was chipped and
> needed to be replaced. And to make matters worse, the machine leaked!
>
> I took it back to the store. I was worried because the machine had
> been on sale, and I had lost my receipt. Luckily, the clerk didn't ask me
> for it. She said a lot of customers had recently had the same problem,
> and she gave me a better machine at the same price.

_____

_____

_____

_____

_____

_____

_____

_____

_____

6 *Jack will fix it!*

A Match each problem with the repair needed.

JACK'S REPAIR SHOP

Item	Problem	Repair needed
1. dishwasher	doesn't work __f__	a. tighten and glue the legs
2. DVD player	DVD is stuck _____	b. repair the wire
3. speakers	wire is damaged _____	c. remove the DVD
4. TV	screen is cracked _____	d. repaint the door
5. stove	metal door is scratched _____	e. replace the screen
6. table	legs are loose _____	✓ f. check the motor

B Write a sentence describing each problem. Then add a sentence describing the action needed to fix it. Use passive infinitives or gerunds.

1. The dishwasher doesn't work. The motor needs to be checked. OR
   The motor needs checking.

2. _____

3. _____

4. _____

5. _____

6. _____

C Think of three items you own that are damaged (or were damaged) in some way. Write a sentence describing each problem. Then write another sentence describing the action needed to fix it.

1. _____

2. _____

3. _____

7 ▪ *Complete the crossword puzzle.*

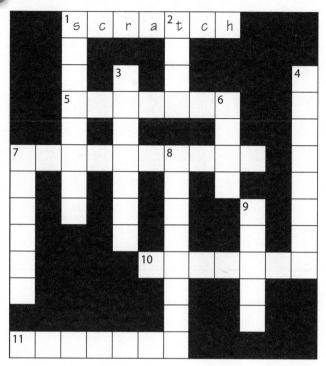

Across

1 My new glasses already have a _____ on one of the lenses.
How did that happen?

5 Your computer screen is so dirty. It needs to be _____ .

7 Something is wrong with your TV screen. It keeps _____ .
It's time to get a new one.

10 I hate this printer. It keeps _____ . The copies won't come out.

11 Be careful – your cup is _____ . I don't want you to cut yourself.

Down

1 The buttons on this remote control keep _____ .
Do you have something to clean it with?

2 Do you realize your jeans are _____ in the back?

3 Your bathroom faucet keeps _____ . Do you want me to try and fix it?

4 This cell phone is driving me crazy! My calls keep _____ .

6 There is a small _____ on the side of my car, but I don't think I'll
bother fixing it.

7 Did your laptop _____ again? I find that so annoying.

8 This old scanner doesn't work at all anymore. It needs to be _____ .

9 The battery in my cell phone keeps _____ . I should buy a new one.

7 The world we live in

1 *Use the information in the pamphlet and the verbs and prepositions given below to change the sentences from the active to the passive.*

HERE ARE JUST SOME OF THE DANGERS FACING YOU AND YOUR CHILDREN.

The water we drink
1. Agricultural runoff is contaminating the water supply.
2. Chlorine and other additives have ruined the taste of our drinking water.

The food we eat
3. Certain agricultural pesticides have caused new illnesses.
4. Pollution from cars and trucks is destroying our crops.

The air we breathe
5. Factories are releasing dangerous chemicals.
6. Breathing smog every day has damaged many people's health.

The world we live in
7. The lack of rainfall has created more severe droughts.
8. Global warming is threatening our forests and wildlife.

Join Save Our Planet Today

1. The water supply is being contaminated due to agricultural runoff. _____ (due to)

2. _____
    _____ (by)

3. _____
    _____ (by)

4. _____
    _____ (because of)

5. _____
    _____ (by)

6. _____
    _____ (as a result of)

7. _____
    _____ (through)

8. _____
    _____ (by)

A Complete the chart.

Verb	Noun	Verb	Noun
contaminate	contamination	educate	_____
contribute	_____	_____	pollution
_____	creation	populate	_____
deplete	_____	protect	_____
_____	destruction	_____	reduction

B Write four sentences like the ones in Exercise 1 using words from the chart.

Example: <u>Many rivers and streams have been badly contaminated by industrial waste.</u>

1. _____

2. _____

3. _____

4. _____

3 *Choose the correct words or phrases.*

1. Green organizations are trying to save rain forests that have been _____<u>threatened</u>_____ by developers and farmers. (created / ruined / threatened)

2. One way to inform the public about factories that pollute the environment is through _____ programs on TV. (agricultural / educational / industrial)

3. In many countries of the world, threatened animal and plant species are being _____ by strict laws. (created / polluted / protected)

4. Agricultural pesticides are _____ the soil in many countries. (damaging / eating up / lowering)

5. _____ is an enormous problem in many large cities where whole families can only afford to live in one room. (pollution / poverty / waste)

El Yunque rain forest

How safe are your plastic cards?

A Scan the first paragraph of this article about plastic cards. Why are more and more people using these cards? Can you think of any other reasons?

It's in the cards.

Nowadays, many people pay for things with credit cards. Six billion cards are produced worldwide annually, and the number is increasing year by year. Bills and coins are gradually being replaced by "plastic money." Banks are issuing debit cards, and charge cards are being offered by many types of stores and businesses. People are now using plastic cards in supermarkets, at gas stations, and for public transportation in many countries around the world. In addition, cards that used to be made of paper are being replaced by plastic ones. For example, many gym membership cards are now made of plastic.

How safe is the plastic used to make these cards? Most cards are made from a plastic called polyvinyl chloride (PVC). While PVC is being produced, harmful chemicals are released into the atmosphere. One of the most dangerous chemicals released is dioxin, which is known to cause cancer in humans. Another problem is that PVC cards are not biodegradable; in other words, when they are thrown away, they do not "break down" and cannot be recycled.

So, why is PVC still being used to make credit cards? Over recent years, research has been done to try to find safer and biodegradable materials to produce plastic money. However, none of the alternatives currently available is sustainable, and all of them are very expensive. For instance, paper cards are more eco-friendly to produce than PVC because they can be recycled. The problem is that they often do not last until their expiration dates. When they get wet, they biodegrade immediately. Paper cards, therefore, have to be replaced frequently, which is expensive. Research has been done with cards made of wood, but it's difficult to make wood both flexible and unbreakable. Some people have suggested metal, but others say it's dangerous to put metal objects into electronic equipment.

Recently, a polylactic acid (PLA) has been suggested as a material for credit cards. It's a bio-based polymer made from corn. In 2009, three Japanese companies – Mitsubishi Plastic, Dai Nippon Printing, and Sony – announced the development of the first credit card made from natural sources approved for use by MasterCard Worldwide, a corporation that processes electronic payments. However, many people complain that, in a world where lots of people are hungry, it's wrong to use a food crop and turn it into plastic.

B Read the article. Check (✓) the true statements. For statements that are false, write the true information.

1. ☐ The plastic used in making most credit cards is fairly safe.

_____

2. ☐ Most plastic cards biodegrade over time.

_____

3. ☐ Paper cards are expensive because they biodegrade very easily.

_____

4. ☐ Research shows that wood and metal are good materials for making cards.

_____

5. ☐ Some companies have issued cards made of polylactic acid.

_____

6. ☐ There are no problems with these new cards.

_____

5 *Nouns beginning with* **over**

A Match the nouns and definitions.

Nouns

1. overbuilding   _e_
2. overcrowding   _____
3. overflowing   _____
4. overfishing   _____
5. overuse   _____
6. overburdened   _____

Definitions

a. putting something to a particular purpose too often

b. catching so many fish that the population is depleted

c. having too much of something to deal with

d. having too many people or things to be contained; spilling over

e. having too many structures and homes in a certain area

f. having too many people or things in a contained area

B Choose the correct noun from part A to complete each sentence.

1. As a result of _____ , we are losing more and more species as well as entire ecosystems.

2. In some major cities, the problem of _____ is a result of too many skyscrapers and too little land area inside the city limits.

3. There is an _____ of fossil fuels when we should be looking for other natural sources of energy like wind and solar power.

4. City officials are trying to stop development in areas with _____ roads and schools.

5. The best way to prevent the _____ of our landfills is to have better and more efficient recycling programs.

6. Another way to help reduce the _____ of our schools is to build more schools and hire more teachers.

6 Complete the conversations. Use the expressions in the box and the information in the list.

> One thing to do . . .   The best way to fight . . .
> Another thing to do . . .   One way to help . . .

- ☑ complain to the Parks Department about it
- ☐ create more government-funded jobs
- ☐ create more public housing projects
- ☐ educate young people about its dangers
- ☐ organize a public meeting to protest the threat to public property
- ☐ report it to the local newspaper
- ☐ donate money to charities that provide shelters and food

1. A: A big housing developer wants to build an apartment complex in Forest Hill Park. I think that's terrible, but what can we do?

   B: _One thing to do is to complain to the Parks Department about it._

   A: That's a good idea.

   B: _____

2. A: Personally, I'm worried about drug trafficking. It puts lots of children and young people at risk.

   B: _____

3. A: You know, there's a lot of corruption in our city government.

   B: _____

   A: Yeah, the bad publicity might help to clean things up a bit.

4. A: There are so many unemployed people in this city. I just don't know what can be done about it.

   B: _____

5. A: What worries me most is the number of homeless people on the streets.

   B: _____

   A: I agree.

   B: _____

a new housing development?

7 *Complete the sentences using the present continuous passive or the present perfect passive. Then suggest a solution to each problem.*

1. Prices <u>have been raised</u> (raise) a lot in recent years.

   One way to deal with inflation <u>is to stop paying raises</u>   .

2. These days, a lot of endangered animals _____ (kill)

   by hunters and poachers. The best way to stop this practice _____

   _____ .

3. During the past few years, lots of trees _____ (destroy)

   by acid rain. One thing to do about it _____

   _____ .

4. Underground water _____ (contaminate)

   by agricultural pesticides. The best way to deal with the problem _____

   _____ .

5. Too many young people's lives _____ (ruin)

   through the use of illegal drugs. The best way to fight drug traffickers _____

   _____ .

8 *Write two paragraphs about a charity, an organization that helps people. In the first paragraph, describe what the charity does. In the second paragraph, explain why you think the charity is useful.*

> A good charity in my city is Shelter. This organization works to reduce the number of homeless people on our streets. Shelter believes the best way to do this is to . . .
>
> Shelter is my favorite charity because homelessness is, in my opinion, the greatest problem facing my city. Many people cannot find jobs, and . . .

_____

_____

_____

_____

_____

_____

_____

8 Lifelong learning

1 *Choose the correct words or phrases.*

1. I'm interested in human behavior, so I'm planning to take a class in _____ .
   (geography / psychology / math)

2. I want to take a course in _____ , such as commerce or accounting. (education / business / social science)

3. I'd prefer not to study _____ because I'm not very comfortable in hospitals.
   (engineering / new media / nursing)

4. I'd really like to work in Information Technology, so I'm thinking of taking courses in _____ .
   (computer science / finance / English)

2 *What would you prefer?*

A Write questions with *would rather* or *would prefer* using the cues.

1. take a science class / an art class

   Would you rather take a science class or an art class?   OR

   Would you prefer to take a science class or an art class?

2. study part time / full time

   _____

3. have a boring job that pays well / an exciting job that pays less

   _____

4. take a long vacation once a year / several short vacations each year

   _____

B Write answers to the questions you wrote in part A.

1. _____
2. _____
3. _____
4. _____

3 *Love it or leave it*

A First, complete speaker A's questions with four things you would *not* like to do. Use ideas in the box or your own ideas.

> learn to play the accordion   study sociology
> learn clothing design   take a class in personal finance
> learn how to repair watches   take a cooking class

Example:

    A: <u>Do you want to learn to play the accordion?</u>

    B: <u>I'd rather not. I'd prefer to take a cooking class.</u>   OR

       <u>I'd prefer not to. I'd rather take a cooking class.</u>

1. A: Do you want to _____ ?

    B: _____

2. A: Would you like to _____ ?

    B: _____

3. A: Do you want to _____ ?

    B: _____

4. A: Would you like to _____ ?

    B: _____

B Now write responses for speaker B. Use the short answers *I'd rather not* or *I'd prefer not to* and say what you would prefer to do.

 4 *Answer these questions and give reasons.*

1. On your day off, would you rather stay home or go out?

   <u>I'd rather stay home than go out because</u> _____

2. Would you prefer to have a cat or a bird?

   _____

3. Would you rather live in the city or the country?

   _____

4. When you entertain friends, would you rather invite them over for dinner or take them out to a restaurant?

   _____

5. Would you prefer to see a new movie at the theater or download it and watch it at home?

   _____

5 Homeschooling

A In some countries, there are children who are educated by their parents at home instead of by teachers at school. Do you think this is a good or a bad idea? Write down two advantages and two disadvantages.

B Read the online newspaper article. Underline the information that answers these questions.

1. How many children in the United States learn at home?
2. Why do some parents prefer to teach their own children?
3. How do the Gutersons choose what to teach their children?
4. What are two criticisms of homeschooling?

Parents . . . and teachers, too! Go to

All children in the United States have to receive an education, but the law does not say they have to be educated in a school. A growing number of parents prefer not to send their children to school. Children who are educated at home are known as "homeschoolers." It is estimated that there are between 1.5 and 1.9 million homeschoolers in the United States today.

Some parents prefer to teach their children at home because they do not believe that schools teach the correct religious values. Others believe they can provide a better education for their children at home. There are now many websites about homeschooling, and many parents who teach their children at home use the Internet to exchange ideas and resources. Interestingly, results show that homeschooled children often do better than average on national tests in reading and math.

David Guterson and his wife teach their three children at home. Guterson says that his children learn very differently from children in school. A lesson starts with the children's interests and questions. If the Brazilian rain forests are in the news, it could start a discussion about how rain forests influence the climate, how deserts are formed, and how the polar ice caps affect ocean levels.

Homeschooling is often more interesting than going to a traditional school, but critics say that homeschoolers can become social outsiders who are uncomfortable mixing with other people in adult life. Another criticism is that many parents are not well qualified to teach. However, most parents don't have the time or the desire to teach their children at home, so most children still get their education at school.

C What could the Gutersons teach their children if the TV news showed . . . ?

1. people without enough food to eat _____

_____

2. a space robot landing on Mars _____

_____

3. doctors announcing a cure for the common cold _____

_____

D After reading the newspaper article, would you make any changes to the advantages and disadvantages you listed in part A?

6 Complete the sentences with **by** + *gerund.* Use **not** *if needed.*
Use the ideas in the box or your own information.

cook at home	eat out	go out more often	study dance
eat good food	exercise regularly	stay home	use social networks

cook at home

study dance

use social networks

1. A good way to enjoy the weekend is <u>not by staying home but by going out with friends.</u>

2. A good way to keep in touch with old friends is _____

3. You can make new friends _____

4. The best way to save money is _____

5. You could stay in shape _____

6. I stay healthy _____

7. One way to learn self-confidence is _____

7 Choose the correct words or phrases.

1. Miriam shows her _____ by volunteering to help people
   with cancer. (competitiveness / communication skills / concern for others)

2. My parents' love of art, poetry, and music taught me _____
   from a very young age. (artistic appreciation / cooperation / perseverance)

3. I learned _____ from my parents. They taught me the importance of being
   polite to both family and friends. (creativity / courtesy / self-confidence)

4. Barbara always gets upset with people who disagree with her. I wish she would show
   more _____ . (perseverance / self-confidence / tolerance)

5. I recently joined a choir, and I love it. But you need a lot of _____ ,
   because you have to practice the same piece of music for weeks before you're
   ready to perform it! (cooperation / perseverance / volunteering)

8 Personal qualities

A Read about each student in these descriptions and choose a suitable quality for each one.

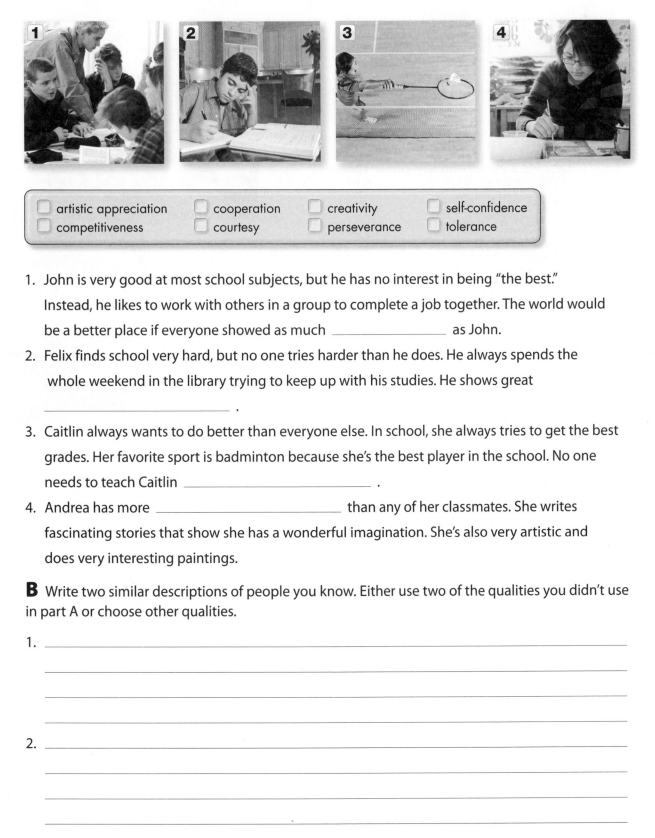

- ☐ artistic appreciation
- ☐ competitiveness
- ☐ cooperation
- ☐ courtesy
- ☐ creativity
- ☐ perseverance
- ☐ self-confidence
- ☐ tolerance

1. John is very good at most school subjects, but he has no interest in being "the best." Instead, he likes to work with others in a group to complete a job together. The world would be a better place if everyone showed as much _____ as John.

2. Felix finds school very hard, but no one tries harder than he does. He always spends the whole weekend in the library trying to keep up with his studies. He shows great

   _____ .

3. Caitlin always wants to do better than everyone else. In school, she always tries to get the best grades. Her favorite sport is badminton because she's the best player in the school. No one needs to teach Caitlin _____ .

4. Andrea has more _____ than any of her classmates. She writes fascinating stories that show she has a wonderful imagination. She's also very artistic and does very interesting paintings.

B Write two similar descriptions of people you know. Either use two of the qualities you didn't use in part A or choose other qualities.

1. _____

   _____

   _____

   _____

2. _____

   _____

   _____

   _____

9 *My way*

A List two methods of learning each of these skills.

1. become a good guitarist

   <u>by teaching myself</u>

   <u>by taking lessons</u>

2. improve my writing ability in English

3. become a more confident public speaker

4. learn more about personal finance

5. become skilled at auto repair

6. learn a new computer program

my first guitar

ten years later

B Which of the two methods in part A would you prefer to use to develop each skill? Write sentences using *would rather (not)* or *would prefer (not)*. Give reasons.

1. <u>I'd rather learn guitar by teaching myself than by taking lessons.</u>

   <u>I'd prefer not to take lessons because they're expensive.</u>

2.

3.

4.

5.

6.

Improvements

1 *Which service does each person need? Choose the correct word or phrase.*

- ☐ dry cleaning
- ☐ home repairs
- ☐ house painting
- ☐ language tutoring
- ☑ lawn mowing
- ☐ pet-sitting

1. lawn mowing

   Marty: I have a new home and don't have much time for yard work. I mowed the lawn two weeks ago, and I need to cut it again. I'd like to save money, but perhaps I'll just have to pay someone to do it for me.

2. _____

   Junko: I don't like the flowered wallpaper in my bedroom or the dark color of the walls in my living room. I want to have the wallpaper removed so the whole place looks bigger and brighter with fun, modern colors everywhere.

3. _____

   Elizabeth: Now that it's getting colder, I need to take my winter clothes out of storage. Some things I can wash in the washing machine, but I should take my wool coat to that new place around the corner.

4. _____

   David: Do you know anyone who can take care of my cat? I'm going on a two-week trip. Actually, I'd prefer someone to come to my apartment every day to play with him and feed him while I'm gone. Yeah, that's a better idea!

5. _____

   Bill: I'm so excited! I'm finally going to Quebec this summer. I studied French in high school, but I'm not sure how much I remember now. Do you know anyone who can help me improve my French?

6. _____

   Paula: I really want to move into that studio apartment I found downtown. The only problem is that there are a lot of little things that need to be repaired. Where can I get a leaky faucet and a broken lock repaired?

home repairs

language tutoring

lawn mowing

2 Where can I get . . . ?

A Match the verbs in column A with the nouns in column B.

A	B	
☑ check	☐ a stain	1. <u>check my blood pressure</u>
☐ cut	☑ my blood pressure	2. _____
☐ do	☐ my computer	3. _____
☐ fix	☐ my hair	4. _____
☐ print	☐ my nails	5. _____
☐ remove	☐ my pants	6. _____
☐ shorten	☐ my photos	7. _____

B First, use the items in part A to write *Where can I get . . . ?* or *Where can I have . . . ?* questions for speaker A. Then write responses for speaker B using your own ideas.

1. A: <u>Where can I get my blood pressure checked?</u>

   B: <u>You can get it checked at the King Street Clinic.</u>

2. A: _____

   B: _____

3. A: _____

   B: _____

4. A: _____

   B: _____

5. A: _____

   B: _____

6. A: _____

   B: _____

7. A: _____

   B: _____

3 *Where can you have these services done? Write sentences with* **You can have . . . .**

1. <u>You can have your hair cut at Salon 21.</u>

2. _____

3. _____

4. _____

5. _____

6. _____

7. _____

8. _____

A Look at the picture. How would you feel working there? Why? What about the design and layout of the room would affect how well you work there?

Feng Shui

For thousands of years, the ancient art form of feng shui has played a major role in Chinese life. Feng shui means "wind and water," and it is based on an appreciation of the relationship between people and the environment. It involves changing the design of your living or working space to improve your fortune.

Soon after a Hong Kong millionaire moved his company to a new skyscraper, his business began to do badly. He called in feng shui experts, who told him that because his new building was round, it was like a cigarette – all the energy was burning off through the roof. They said that the only thing he could do to prevent this was to build a swimming pool on the roof. He followed their advice, and his business started to do well again.

In another case, retail giant Marks & Spencer performed poorly when it entered the Chinese market with the opening of its store in Shanghai.

Within days of opening in 2008, the new store was in serious trouble. Shoppers were unimpressed. Within three months, the man in charge of opening the store in the Chinese city had been fired. What was the cause of Marks & Spencer's problems? While some blame bad planning, many locals say the building simply has bad feng shui. The principles were not respected in building the store.

In recent years, feng shui has become popular in many western countries where companies such as Nike, Citibank, and Hyatt Hotels have started to seek advice from experts. Coca-Cola's headquarters in Atlanta reported an increase in profits and employee efficiency after using feng shui principles in its new offices. So does the business world believe in feng shui? Some people do, but others just see it as good business. As one real estate developer said, "I don't have to believe in feng shui; I do it because it makes me money."

B Read the article about feng shui. Check (✓) the true statements.
For statements that are false, write the true information.

1. ☐ Feng shui concerns the relationship between humans and the world around them.

_____

2. ☐ According to feng shui, a round building is good for business.

_____

3. ☐ Feng shui has been popular in western countries for several centuries.

_____

4. ☐ Marks & Spencer used feng shui in designing its Shanghai store.

_____

5. ☐ Coca-Cola's headquarters reported an increase in employee efficiency after using feng shui principles in its new offices.

_____

5 *Write two suggestions for each of these problems.*

1. I never have any energy, so I can never do anything except work. I sleep all weekend, so don't tell me to get more rest! Have you thought about <u>taking an aerobics class?</u>
<u>Another option is improve your diet.</u>

2. My problem is a constant backache. I just don't know what to do to get rid of it. I had someone give me a massage, but it didn't really help.
Maybe you could _____
_____

3. My doctor told me to get more exercise. She strongly recommended swimming, but I find swimming so boring! In fact, aren't all sports boring?
Why don't you _____
_____

4. I'm very sociable, and I have great difficulty saying no. I end up doing things every night of the week – going to parties, clubs, the movies. I'm so tired all the time!
It might be a good idea _____
_____

5. I like to be a good neighbor, but the woman next door drives me crazy. She's always knocking on my door to chat. And whenever I go out into the yard, she goes into her yard – and talks for hours!
What about _____
_____

6 *Choose the correct three-word phrasal verb for each sentence.*

1. I don't know how my grandmother _____ all the new
   technology. She's better at understanding new gadgets than I am!
   (comes up with / cuts down on / keeps up with)

2. My cousin didn't know what to do for her mother's 60th birthday, but she finally
   _____ the idea of a surprise picnic with the whole family.
   (came up with / got along with / looked forward to)

3. Judy has done it again! She only met Sam two months ago, and already she has
   _____ him. Why doesn't she try to work out any problems?
   (broken up with / gotten along with / kept up with)

4. After Pat saw her doctor, she decided to _____ eating fast
   food. She wants to lose some weight and start exercising again in order to keep
   fit. (cut down on / look forward to / take care of)

5. We're really lucky in my family because we all _____
   each other very well. (come up with / get along with / look forward to)

6. I've done pretty badly in my classes this semester, so I'm not really _____
   receiving my grades. (getting along with / looking forward to / taking care of)

7. I can't _____ that loud music anymore! I can't stand hip-hop,
   and I'm going to tell my neighbor right now. (cut down on / put up with /
   take care of)

8. I've been getting sick a lot lately, and I often feel tired. I really need to start
   _____ my health. (cutting down on / keeping up
   with / taking care of)

The past and the future

1 Circle the correct word that describes each sentence.

1. Events in December 2010 led to the peaceful removal of Tunisia's prime minister in January 2011. (natural disaster / epidemic / revolution)

2. In 2009, a species of spider that eats plants was found in southern Mexico and Central America. (discovery / invention / epidemic)

3. On March 11, 2004, a series of bombings on a commuter train line in Madrid, Spain, killed 191 people and wounded 1,800. (invention / terrorist act / achievement)

4. Advances in space technology allowed a spacecraft to land on Mars in 1997. (achievement / disaster / terrorist act)

5. Prime Minister Benazir Bhutto of Pakistan was killed after leaving a campaign rally in December 2007. (assassination / election / revolution)

6. In 2010, a series of floods in Australia affected over 200,000 people and caused nearly a billion Australian dollars in damage. (discovery / natural disaster / epidemic)

2 Complete the sentences. Use words from the box.

ago	for	from	in	since	to

1. Jazz first became popular ____in____ the 1920s.

2. The cell phone was invented about 40 years _____ .

3. Brasília has been the capital city of Brazil _____ 1960.

4. The first laptop was produced _____ 1981.

5. Mexico has been independent _____ more than 200 years.

6. World War II lasted _____ 1939 _____ 1945.

7. Vietnam was separated into two parts _____ about 20 years.

8. East and West Germany have been united _____ 1990.

jazz

Brasília

3 *Nouns and verbs*

A Complete this chart. Then check your answers in a dictionary.

Noun	Verb	Noun	Verb
achievement	achieve	existence	
assassination		exploration	
demonstration		explosion	
discovery		invention	
discrimination		transformation	
election		vaccination	

B Choose verbs from the chart in part A to complete these sentences. Use the correct verb tense.

1. Over the past several decades, the Indian city of Bangalore has _____transformed_____ itself into a high-tech center.

2. In World War I, many soldiers were _____ against typhoid, a deadly bacterial disease.

3. Aung San, the man who led Myanmar to independence, was _____ in 1947. No one is certain who killed him.

4. The European Union has _____ since 1957. There are now 27 member states.

5. Until the 1960s, there were many laws that _____ against African Americans in certain regions of the United States.

6. In 1885, Louis Pasteur _____ a cure for rabies when he treated a young boy who was bitten by a dog.

7. In recent years, teams of experts in countries such as Cambodia and Angola have been safely _____ land mines in order to rid those countries of these dangerous weapons.

8. One of the few parts of the world that has not been _____ much is Antarctica. The extreme climate makes it dangerous to travel far from research centers.

Bangalore, a high-tech center

a research station in Antarctica

4 Vaccines past, present, and future

A What are vaccinations? If necessary, scan the article to find out.

Vaccinations

For well over a thousand years, smallpox was a disease that everyone feared. The disease killed much of the native population in South America when the Spanish arrived there in the early sixteenth century. By the end of the eighteenth century, smallpox was responsible for the deaths of about one in ten people around the world. Those who survived the disease were left with ugly scars on their skin.

It had long been well known among farmers that people who worked with cows rarely caught smallpox; instead, they often caught a similar but much milder disease called cowpox. A British doctor named Edward Jenner was fascinated by this, and so he studied cowpox. He became convinced that, by injecting people with cowpox, he could protect them against the much worse disease smallpox. In 1796, he vaccinated a boy with cowpox and, two months later, with smallpox. The boy did not get smallpox. In the next two years, Jenner vaccinated several children in the same way, and none of them got the disease.

News of Jenner's success soon spread. In 1800, the Royal Vaccine Institution was founded in Berlin,

Germany. In the following year, Napoleon opened a similar institute in Paris, France. Vaccination soon became a common method to protect people against other viral diseases, such as rabies, and vaccines were sent across the world to the United States and India.

It took nearly two centuries to achieve Jenner's dream of ridding the world of smallpox. In 1967, the World Health Organization (WHO) started an ambitious vaccination program, and the last known case of smallpox was recorded in Somalia in 1977. The story of vaccinations does not end there, however. There are many other diseases that kill more and more people every year. In addition, many new diseases are being discovered. The challenge for medical researchers will, therefore, probably continue for several more centuries.

B Read the article about vaccinations. Complete the chart with the history of events in the story of vaccinations.

Date	Event
1. Early 16th century	Smallpox killed much of the native population in South America.
2. End of the 18th century	
3. 1796	
4. 1800	
5. 1801	
6. 1967	
7. 1977	
8. Future challenge	

5 Life in 2050

A Complete these predictions about life in 2050. Use the future continuous of the verb given. Then add two more predictions of your own.

life on the moon?

By 2050, . . .

1. some people _will be living_ _____
   in cities on the moon. (live)

2. many people _____
   temperature-controlled body suits. (wear)

3. most people _____
   cars that run on fuel from garbage. (drive)

4. people _____
   in a new Olympic event – mind reading. (compete)

5. _____
   _____

6. _____
   _____

B Complete these predictions about what will have happened by 2050. Use the future perfect. Then add two more predictions of your own.

By 2050, . . .

1. computers _will have replaced_ _____ people
   as translators. (replace)

2. ties for men _____ out
   of fashion. (go)

3. scientists _____ a cheap
   way of getting drinking water from seawater. (discover)

4. medical researchers _____ a cure
   for cancer. (find)

5. _____
   _____

6. _____
   _____

a cure for cancer?

6 *Write two responses to each question.*

1. What will or won't you be doing in ten years? (Use the future continuous.)

   <u>I won't be living with my parents.</u>

   _____

   _____

2. How will cities of the future be different? (Use *will*.)

   <u>Cities won't allow cars downtown.</u>

   _____

   _____

3. How will life in small villages in your country have changed in the next 20 years?
   (Use the future perfect.)

   <u>More people will have moved back from cities to small villages.</u>

   _____

   _____

4. How do you think the world's weather will change during this century? (Use *will*.)

   <u>The weather will be warmer, and the summers will be longer.</u>

   _____

   _____

5. What advances will scientists have made by 2050? (Use the future perfect.)

   <u>Scientists will have found a way to grow enough food for everyone.</u>

   _____

   _____

7 *Think of four ways that technology will affect how we live and work in the next 20 years.*

Example: <u>Robots will be cleaning our homes.</u>

1. _____

2. _____

3. _____

4. _____

8 *Write two paragraphs about one of these topics or a topic of your choice. In the first paragraph, describe the past. In the second paragraph, describe how you think the future will be.*

Topics		
a music group	health	changes within a country
space exploration	changes within a region	technology

> The European Union, or E.U., began as the European Economic Community in 1957. At first, there were only six member states, including France, Italy, and West Germany. Nine other countries joined during the next 40 years. Many European nations came together because they wanted to avoid another world war.
>
> The E.U. has continued to develop during the twenty-first century. In 2002, nearly all the member states adopted the same currency – the euro. In 2004, ten more countries joined the E.U., and two more countries, Romania and Bulgaria, joined in 2007. In the future, the nations of the E.U. will continue to develop economic, political, and social cooperation. In the near future, several more countries, such as Croatia, Iceland, and Turkey, will probably join the E.U.

_____

_____

_____

_____

_____

_____

_____

Life's little lessons

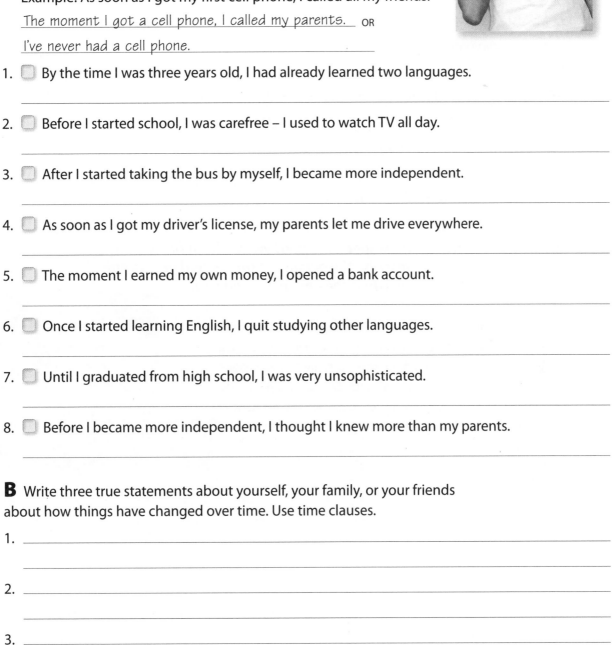

1 Milestones

A Read these statements. Check (✓) the ones that are true for you. For statements that are false, write the true information.

> Example: As soon as I got my first cell phone, I called all my friends.
> <u>The moment I got a cell phone, I called my parents.</u>   OR
> <u>I've never had a cell phone.</u>

1. ☐ By the time I was three years old, I had already learned two languages.
   _____

2. ☐ Before I started school, I was carefree – I used to watch TV all day.
   _____

3. ☐ After I started taking the bus by myself, I became more independent.
   _____

4. ☐ As soon as I got my driver's license, my parents let me drive everywhere.
   _____

5. ☐ The moment I earned my own money, I opened a bank account.
   _____

6. ☐ Once I started learning English, I quit studying other languages.
   _____

7. ☐ Until I graduated from high school, I was very unsophisticated.
   _____

8. ☐ Before I became more independent, I thought I knew more than my parents.
   _____

B Write three true statements about yourself, your family, or your friends about how things have changed over time. Use time clauses.

1. _____
   _____

2. _____
   _____

3. _____
   _____

2 *Complete these descriptions. Use words from the box.*

| ☐ ambitious | ☐ carefree | ☐ rebellious |
| ☐ argumentative | ☐ naive | ☑ sophisticated |

1. Kate is so _____sophisticated_____ . She always dresses well, she knows lots of intelligent people, and she never says anything silly.

2. I just spent a horrible evening with Kendra. She questioned and criticized everything I said. I wish she weren't so _____ .

3. My sister is very _____ . She trusts everyone and thinks everyone is good.

4. Once I turned 16, I became less _____ , and my parents started to let me do what I wanted.

5. Paul is really _____ . He wants to own his own business by the time he's 25.

6. I wish I could be like Celia. She's so _____ and never seems to worry about anything.

3 *Do you have a friend who is special to you? Write about him or her. In the first paragraph, describe the person. In the second paragraph, describe a particular time when the person helped you.*

> One of my best friends is Christine. She's very mature and conscientious, and she always gives me good advice. Until I met her, I had been making some bad decisions. . . .
>
> Christine is also very generous. She always helps her friends when they need it. For example, the moment she found out I was sick last winter, she came over and visited me.

_____

_____

_____

_____

_____

_____

_____

_____

A Scan the article from a sports magazine about Mercy Cherono. What lesson did she learn very quickly?

Learning Quickly from Mistakes

Mercy Cherono is one of many very successful young athletes from Kenya. She was born in 1991 in the village of Kipajit. She is the oldest of six children, and some of her younger siblings are also athletes. Her father, John Koech, runs a training camp in the village. During the school holidays, the camp attracts over 50 trainees.

Cherono started running in primary school and continued when she went to secondary school in the nearby town of Sotik. At the age of 16, she participated in her first international event in Mombasa, Kenya. It was the 2007 International Association of Athletics Federations (IAAF) World Cross Country Championships. She finished 23rd in the junior race, but she had **launched herself into** international athletics. In the same year, at the World Youth Championships at Ostrava in the Czech Republic, she won a gold medal in the 3,000-meter race, which she ran in the championship **record time** of 8:53:94.

In the coming years, she continued to win gold medals at **prestigious** international championships. She is a two-time World Junior Champion in the 3,000-meter race, winning in Poland in 2008, and again in Canada in 2010. She also came in first in the 3,000-meter race at the 2009 Africa Junior Championships. However, Cherono is not just a middle-distance runner. At the 2009 World Cross Country Championships in Jordan, she won a silver medal in the junior race. She lost to the Ethiopian long-distance runner Genzebe Dibaba because she tried to **sprint** too early to the finishing line. After the race, Cherono claimed, "I will not repeat that mistake again."

The following year, at the same cross country race, Cherono proved herself when she won a gold medal. Incredibly, the three **runners-up** were all from Kenya, too. She and the Kenyan team came home to a hero's welcome. Her coach was **ecstatic** and said, "The success of the Kenyan team was through training hard and determination." And her father said, "Our child is a disciplined girl who has always taken instructions." Perhaps one day Mercy Cherono will instruct future champions.

B Read the article. Look at the words and phrases in **bold** in the article. Write definitions or synonyms for each word or phrase.

1. launched herself into _____

2. record time _____

3. prestigious _____

4. sprint _____

5. runners-up _____

6. ecstatic _____

C What factors mentioned in the article do you think have helped Mercy Cherono to become a successful athlete?

5 *Write sentences about your regrets. Use* **should (not) have.**

1. I spent all my money on clothes. Now I can't afford to take a vacation.
   I shouldn't have spent all my money on clothes.

2. I was very argumentative with my boss, so she fired me.
   _____

3. I changed jobs. Now I work in a bank. My job isn't very interesting.
   _____

4. I bought a new TV with my credit card. Now I can't afford the payments.
   _____

5. I studied music in school, but I'm much better at computer science.
   _____

6. I was completely rebellious when I was a student, so I got very bad grades.
   _____

7. My friend asked to copy my homework, so I let him. The teacher found out and
   gave us both Fs.
   _____

8. My cousin invited me to a party. I accepted but didn't put the date in my calendar.
   I forgot all about it.
   _____

9. I was very naive when I was younger. I lent money to people, but they hardly
   ever paid me back.
   _____

10. My friend asked for my opinion on her new hairstyle. I told her I didn't like it.
    Now she's not talking to me.
    _____

6 *If . . .*

A Rewrite the sentences as hypothetical situations. Use the words given.

1. I should have studied English sooner. (get a better job)

   If I'd studied English sooner, I would have gotten a better job.

2. We should have made a reservation. (eat already)

   _____

3. I should have put on sunscreen. (not get a sunburn)

   _____

4. You should have let me drive. (arrive by now)

   _____

5. I should have ignored your text in class. (not get in trouble)

   _____

B Write sentences describing hypothetical situations.
Use the words given and your own ideas.

1. selfish If I had been less selfish as a teenager,

   I would have had a better relationship with my brother.

2. ambitious _____

   _____

3. pragmatic _____

   _____

4. naive _____

   _____

5. rebellious _____

   _____

6. conscientious _____

   _____

Complete the conversation. Circle the correct time expressions and use the correct tense of the verbs given.

Andy: I've made such a mess of my life!

John: What do you mean?

Andy: If I _____hadn't accepted_____
(not accept)

a job ((as soon as)/ before / until) I graduated,

I _____
(travel)

around Europe all summer – just like you

did. You were so carefree.

John: You know, I should _____
(not go)

to Europe. I should _____
(take)

the great job I was offered. (After / Before / Until)

I returned from Europe, it was too late.

Andy: But my job is so depressing! (Before / The moment / Until) I started it,

I hated it – on the very first day! That was five years ago, and nothing's changed.

I should _____ for another job right away.
(look)

John: Well, start looking now. I posted my résumé online last month, and five

companies contacted me right away. If I _____
(not post)

my résumé, no one _____ me.
(contact)

I accepted one of the job offers.

Andy: Really? What's the job?

John: It's working as a landscape gardener. (Before / The moment / Until)

I saw it, I knew it was right for me.

Andy: But for me right now, the problem is that I get a very good salary and I

just bought a house. If I _____ the house,
(not buy)

I _____ take a lower paying job.
(be able to)

John: Well, I guess you can't have everything. If I _____ a better salary,
(have)

I _____ a house, too.
(buy)

12 The right stuff

1 *Complete these sentences with* **In order for** *or* **In order to.**

1. <u>In order for</u> a restaurant to be popular, it has to have attractive decor.

2. _____ a movie to be entertaining, it has to have good actors and an interesting story.

3. _____ succeed in business, you often have to work long hours.

4. _____ attract new members, a sports club needs to offer inexpensive memberships.

5. _____ speak a foreign language well, it's a good idea to use the language as often as possible.

6. _____ a clothing store to succeed, it has to be able to find the latest fashions.

a popular restaurant

2 *Write sentences. Use the information in the box.*

- ☐ have talented salespeople
- ☑ keep up with your studies
- ☐ be clever and entertaining
- ☐ work extremely long hours
- ☐ provide excellent customer service
- ☐ have drama and interesting characters

1. be a successful student

   <u>In order to be a successful student, you have to keep up with your studies.</u>

2. a clothes store to be profitable

   <u>For a clothes store to be profitable,</u> _____

3. manage your own business

   _____

4. an advertisement to be persuasive

   _____

5. run a successful automobile company

   _____

6. a reality TV show to be successful

   _____

3 *Choose the correct word or phrase.*

1. I didn't enjoy this book on how to succeed in business. It wasn't very

   _____well written_____ . (affordable / well paid / well written)

2. I learned a lot about how to run a successful bookstore from taking that class.

   I found it very _____ . (attractive / informative / knowledgeable)

3. Linda has so many interesting ideas, and she's always thinking of new projects.

   She's very _____ . (clever / patient / tough)

4. Rosie is a salesperson, and she's good at her job. She's so _____ that

   she sells three times as much as her co-workers. (unfriendly / affordable / persuasive)

5. Daniel is one of the top models in Milan. He goes to the gym every day, so

   he looks really _____ . (clever / charming / muscular)

6. For a restaurant to succeed, it has to _____ a high level of

   quality in both food and service. (keep up with / maintain / put up with)

7. If a department store improves its _____ and looks really

   fashionable, it can attract a lot of new customers. (boutique / decor / safety record)

4 *Read this information about journalists. Then write a paragraph about one of the people in the box or another person of your choice.*

> To be a successful journalist, you need to be both talented and dynamic. You have to write well and write quickly. In order to report the news, a journalist needs to have a good knowledge of world and current events. In addition, you must be able to report a story accurately.

| an artist   a boss   a homemaker   a parent   a teacher |

_____

_____

_____

_____

_____

_____

A For each pair of pictures, write one sentence about what you like and one sentence about what you dislike. Give reasons using the words given.

1

I like this park because it's clean

and there are a lot of trees. _____ **(because)**

I don't like this park since _____

_____ **(since)**

2

_____

_____ **(since)**

_____

_____ **(the reason)**

3

_____

_____ **(because of)**

_____

_____ **(due to)**

B Think of an example in your city of each of these places: a restaurant, a hotel, a shopping center. Write a sentence about why you like or dislike each one.

Example: _The reason I don't like Cho Dang Gol Restaurant in my hometown_

is its noisy location right by the freeway.

1. _____

2. _____

3. _____

A Scan the article about Muji. What is the company's philosophy?

BUSINESS AS UNUSUAL

From very small beginnings over three decades ago, Muji is now well-known for its stores in East Asia, Europe, and North America. It is proud to operate in a very unique way. Exactly how does this international chain store's philosophy differ from that of its **competitors**?

The answer can be found in its full Japanese name, Mujirushi Ryohin, which means "no brand quality goods." The company's **basic principle** is to provide new but simple products at "lower than usual prices" by maximizing the use of the most suitable **raw materials** available. In order to achieve this, Muji selects the best materials and then, in the manufacturing process, it minimizes waste, often by recycling unused materials. Another key concept at Muji concerns using **minimal packaging** showing only product-related information and a price tag.

When Muji was established in Japan in 1980, it operated only in "sales corners" in department stores and convenience stores, such as Seibu and Family Mart. It sold 31 food items, ranging from dried shiitake mushrooms to fruit drinks. There were nine items for kitchens and bathrooms, such as phosphorus-free detergent and toothbrushes. Muji expanded quickly. In 1983, the company founded its own stores and extended its **product range** to include fabrics – curtains, bed linens, and clothes. It also began opening shops abroad and now has hundreds

of stores in countries as far apart as the United States, Turkey, and China. Moreover, to keep up with the electronic shopping revolution, Muji Online enables customers to place orders from home.

Over the years, Muji products have won several product design awards. For instance, in 2005, Muji won several gold awards at the International Forum Design in Germany. When the company organized its own design awards the following year, it attracted 4,758 entries from 52 countries.

The bottom line at Muji is to offer well-designed, high-quality, logo-free products at tempting prices. It works!

B Read the article. Look at the words and phrases in **bold** in the article. Write definitions or synonyms for each word or phrase.

1. competitors _____

2. basic principle _____

3. raw materials _____

4. minimal packaging _____

5. product range _____

6. the bottom line _____

7 *Look at these advertisements and write two sentences about each one. Describe the features and give reasons why you like or dislike the advertisements.*

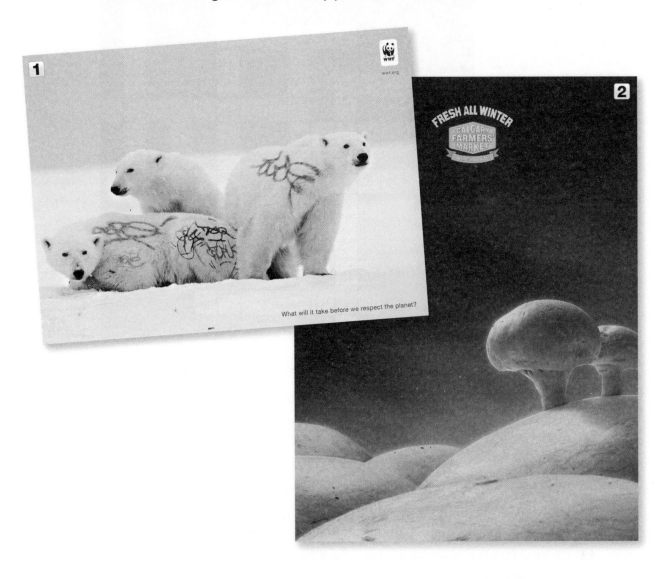

Example: <u>A nice thing about the first ad is that it attracts your attention.</u>

<u>I like it because of the clever concept.</u>

1. _____

_____

_____

2. _____

_____

_____

8 *Complete this crossword puzzle.*

Across

3 For a salesperson to be persuasive, he or she has to be _____ with words.

5 The big supermarket _____ are causing many small local stores to close.

7 In order for sports clubs to remain popular, they must have the most modern _____ , such as treadmills and stair climbers.

9 To be _____ , successful male models work out daily with trainers.

10 I don't follow trends, so the latest _____ in clothes don't interest me.

12 I don't have a favorite _____ of clothing. Designer clothes are too expensive, so I just buy cheap clothes that look good on me.

13 I like the family-owned shop on my street because it always has interesting _____ products that I've never seen before.

14 I don't know why Gloria doesn't try modeling. She is absolutely _____ .

Down

1 For a coffee shop to make enough money to be _____ in my neighborhood, it has to attract young people and stay open late.

2 The Leo Jazz Club has a great new band. I've heard they're very _____ musicians.

4 Due to its boring content, *Weekend Talk* ran for only three months. For a TV show to be successful on Saturday evenings, it really has to be _____ .

6 I wouldn't be a good _____ because I'm not very persuasive.

8 While I was waiting in the doctor's office, I read a fantastic new _____ . I liked it so much that I decided to buy it every month from now on.

11 I'm not _____ enough to be a successful salesperson. When someone says no, I would just accept that, but I'm sure that's not how to make a sale!

13 That's a possibility.

1 *What do you think happened? Write an explanation for each event using past modals.*

1. He may have lost his car key. _____

2. _____

3. _____

4. _____

5. _____

6. _____

  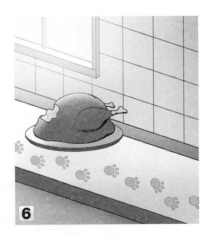

2 *Write two paragraphs about something strange that has happened to you. In the first paragraph, describe the situation. In the second paragraph, give two or three explanations for what happened.*

> I invited six friends to a barbecue on the beach. I suggested we meet at eight o'clock. They all said they would come and bring some food.
>
> On the day of the barbecue, only two of my friends showed up. I guess my other friends could have overslept, or they might have decided to do something else. Another possibility is that they may have thought I meant 8 p.m. instead of 8 a.m. I'm not sure what happened!

_____

_____

_____

_____

_____

_____

_____

_____

3 *Answer these questions. Write two explanations using past modals.*

Why do you think the ancient Britons built Stonehenge?

1. They might have <u>built it to use as a church.</u>

2. _____

How do you think early explorers communicated with people in the places they visited?

3. They could have _____

4. _____

How do you think the early Polynesians were able to travel across vast oceans?

5. They may have _____

6. _____

4 *Strange creatures*

A Skim the online article about a world-famous legend.
Can you think of a suitable title for it?

He has been called the "missing link": half man, half beast. He is huge, maybe as much as 2.5 meters tall (8 feet). His body is covered with long brown hair, but his face is hairless. He walks upright on two feet. He lives near the top of Mount Everest, and he is known as the Abominable Snowman.

The legend of this strange creature is not new. For years, local people have reported seeing the creature they call "Yeti" (the all-eating animal) come down from the mountain and attack villagers. Climbers in the 1920s reported stories of huge footprints they saw high in the Himalayas – footprints unlike any other animal's. In 1951, the explorer Eric Shipton took photographs of enormous tracks in the snow of Mount Everest. He assumed that the Abominable Snowman really existed and must have walked around in that area.

These days, a few people still believe in the Yeti. However, scientists say there should have been more and better evidence than just some footprints in the snow. They also suggest that the tracks Shipton found may have been only bear tracks. However, if anyone ever succeeds in catching an Abominable Snowman, they may face a real problem: Would they put it in a zoo or give it a room in a hotel?

B Read the article. Then write answers to the questions.

1. How might someone describe the Abominable Snowman?

   _____

2. Where does the Abominable Snowman live?

   _____

3. What's another name for the Abominable Snowman?

   _____

4. In 1951, what "evidence" did Shipton find, and how did he record it?

   _____

5. Why don't many scientists believe Shipton found tracks of the Abominable Snowman?

   _____

5 *Should have, could have, would have*

A What should or shouldn't these people have done?
Read each situation and check (✓) the best suggestion.

1. Joe's old car broke down on the highway late one night, and
   his cell phone battery was dead. He left the car on the side
   of the road and walked home.

   ☐ He should have stopped a stranger's car to
     ask for a ride.
   ☐ He could have slept in his car till morning.
   ☐ He should have walked to the nearest
     pay phone and called a tow truck.

2. Linda was in a park. She saw some people leave all their
   trash after they had finished their picnic. She did nothing.

   ☐ She did the right thing.
   ☐ She should have asked them to throw away their trash.
   ☐ She could have thrown away the trash herself.

3. John's neighbors were renovating their kitchen. They made
   a lot of noise every day until midnight. John called the police.

   ☐ He shouldn't have called the police.
   ☐ He should have realized that they were trying
     to finish the job quickly.
   ☐ He could have asked them not to make any noise in the evenings.

4. Mrs. Judd wouldn't let her children watch TV for a month
   because they broke a window playing baseball.

   ☐ She could have made them pay for the window.
   ☐ She shouldn't have done anything. It was an accident.
   ☐ She shouldn't have let them play baseball for a month.

5. Martha's boss borrowed $20 from her a month ago, but he forgot
   to pay her back. Martha never said anything about it.

   ☐ She should have demanded her money back.
   ☐ She shouldn't have loaned it to him.
   ☐ She could have written him a nice email asking for the money.

B What would you have done in the situations in part A?
Write suggestions or comments using past modals.

1. _I would have called a friend to give me a ride home._

2. _____

3. _____

4. _____

5. _____

6 *Nouns and verbs*

A Complete the chart.

Noun	Verb	Noun	Verb
advice	*advise*	excuse	_____
_____	assume	_____	predict
criticism	_____	suggestion	_____
_____	demand	_____	warn

B Complete the sentences using words from the chart in part A. For the verbs, use *shouldn't have* + past participle. For the nouns, use the appropriate singular or plural form.

1. Justin ___shouldn't have suggested___ having a beach party. It was so dark, I stepped in a hole and hurt my ankle.

2. Bart bought an expensive ring and gave it to Millie for her birthday. A year later, he asked her to marry him. When she said no, he made an outrageous _____ . He said he wanted his ring back!

3. I _____ my co-worker not to be late for work so often. It was really none of my business.

4. Last year some economists said that food and gas prices wouldn't increase. Those _____ were wrong! Both food and gas are more expensive now.

5. Jill said she was late because she got caught in traffic. Hmm. I've heard that _____ before.

6. Philip _____ I would still be awake at midnight. I was asleep when he called.

7. My professor _____ me to take a course in English literature. I have absolutely no interest in it.

8. Josh _____ me for wearing jeans and a T-shirt to a friend's party.

That's a possibility. ▪ 77

Complete these conversations. Use the past modals in the box and the verbs given. (More than one modal is possible.)

could have
may have
might have
must have
should have

1. A: Where's Alex? He's late.

   B: He ___may have gotten___ (get) stuck in rush-hour traffic.

   A: He's always late! You know, he ___should have taken___ (take) the subway.

2. A: Nina never responded to my invitation.

   B: She _____ (not receive) it.

   You _____ (call) her.

3. A: Jeff hasn't answered his phone for a week.

   B: He _____ (go) on vacation.

   He _____ (tell) you,

   though – sometimes he's very inconsiderate.

4. A: I can never get in touch with Susan. She never returns phone calls
   or answers texts!

   B: Yeah, I have the same problem with her. Her voice mail

   _____ (run out) of space.

   She _____ (get) a new

   phone service by now.

5. A: Martin is strange. Sometimes he works really hard, but sometimes

   he seems pretty lazy. Last week, he hardly did any work.

   B: Well, you know, he _____ (not feel) well.

   Still, he _____ (tell) you that he was sick.

6. A: I ordered a book online a month ago, but it still hasn't arrived.

   B: They _____ (have) a problem with the

   warehouse, but they _____ (let) you know.

14 Behind the scenes

 1 *Complete the conversation. Use the passive form of the verbs given.*

Vera: Putting on a fashion show must be really challenging!

Isaac: Yeah, but it's also fun. All the clothes have to __be numbered__ (number) so that the models wear them in the right sequence. And they also have to _____ (mark) with the name of the right model.

Vera: What happens if something _____ (wear) by the wrong model?

Isaac: Well, if it doesn't fit, it looks terrible! First impressions are very important. A lot of clothes _____ (sell) because they look good at the show.

Vera: Do you have to rehearse for a fashion show?

Isaac: Of course! There's more involved than just models and clothes. Special lighting _____ (use), and music _____ (play) during the show.

Vera: It sounds complicated.

Isaac: Oh, it is. And at some fashion shows, a commentary may _____ (give).

Vera: A commentary? What do you mean?

Isaac: Well, someone talks about the clothes as they _____ (show) on the runway by the models.

Vera: It sounds like timing is really important.

Isaac: Exactly. Everything has to _____ (time) perfectly! Otherwise, the show may _____ (ruin).

2 *Choose the correct words or phrases.*

1. Often, special music has to be _____ for a film.

   (composed / designed / hired)

2. A play may be _____ for several weeks before it is shown to the public.

   (shot / taken / rehearsed)

3. Designing _____ for actors to wear requires a lot of creativity.

   (scripts / sets / costumes)

4. Newspapers are _____ to stores after they are printed.

   (expanded / distributed / reported)

5. _____ are added after the film has been put together.

   (Scenes / Sound effects / Takes)

3 *Complete this passage. Use the passive form of the verbs given.*

1. Nowadays, all sorts of things ____*are produced*____ (produce) in factories,

   including lettuce! At one food factory, fresh green lettuce _____ (grow)

   without sunlight or soil. Here is how it _____ (do).

2. Lettuce seedlings _____ (place) at one end of a long production line.

   Conveyor belts _____ (use) to move the seedlings slowly along.

   The tiny plants _____ (expose) to light from fluorescent lamps.

3. They have to _____ (feed) through the roots with plant food

   and water that _____ (control) by a computer.

4. Thirty days later, the plants _____ (collect) at the other end

   of the conveyor belts.

5. They may _____ (deliver) to the vegetable market the same day.

A Skim the article. Write the type of puppet under the correct pictures.

INTERNATIONAL PUPPETS

The first puppets are thought to have been used in India over 4,000 years ago. Since then, different kinds of puppets have become popular around the world.

HAND PUPPETS are usually about 50 cm (20 inches) tall. Their main feature is a large head that has a costume with arms attached to it. These puppets are worn like a glove. The puppeteer, who stands below the stage, operates the puppet with his or her fingers. Hand puppets are widely used in European countries, such as Italy, France, and Britain.

ROD PUPPETS have long been used in Japan and Italy and are now very popular in Eastern Europe. They are similar in shape to hand puppets but are much bigger – sometimes over 1 meter (40 inches) tall. The puppeteer, who works from below the stage, operates the puppet with rods that are attached to it: a thick rod fixed to the puppet's back, and thinner rods fixed to its neck, head, and arms. The puppeteer, holding the thick rod in one hand and the thinner rods in the other hand, can move the parts separately.

SHADOW PUPPETS are similar to rod puppets but are unique in that they are flat and much smaller – about 50 cm (20 inches). In addition, they are seen by audiences in a completely different way – these puppets appear as shadows on a screen that is lit from behind. They are controlled either from below or beside the stage. Shadow puppets, which originally came from China and Indonesia, later became popular in Turkey and Greece.

MARIONETTES are puppets that are constructed from several small parts. Their height varies, and they are moved by strings that are controlled from above. Many marionettes are hung on nine strings, but there are some in Myanmar that have up to 60 strings. They can be made to perform interesting tricks, such as blowing smoke from a pipe.

1. _____ 2. _____ 3. _____ 4. _____

B Read the article about different types of puppets. Complete the chart.

	Hand puppets	Rod puppets	Shadow puppets	Marionettes
Size	_____	_____	_____	_____
How they're constructed	_____	_____	_____	_____
	_____	_____	_____	_____
How they're moved	_____	_____	_____	_____
	_____	_____	_____	_____
Position of puppeteer	_____	_____	_____	_____
	_____	_____	_____	_____
Where they're commonly used	_____	_____	_____	_____
	_____	_____	_____	_____

5 *Join these sentences with **who** or **that**. Add a comma wherever one is needed.*

foreign correspondent

junior newspaper reporter

Examples:

Foreign correspondents are journalists.

They report on a particular part of the world.

Foreign correspondents are journalists that report on a particular part of the world.

A junior newspaper reporter should be curious.

He or she is often new to journalism.

A junior newspaper reporter, who is often new to journalism, should be curious.

1. A photo editor selects only the best photos.

   He or she tells the photographers what news stories to cover.

   _____

   _____

2. A website designer is a skilled artist.

   He or she creates computer files with text, sound, and graphics.

   _____

   _____

3. A network installer is a skilled person.

   He or she responds to calls from people with computer problems.

   _____

   _____

4. Movie extras appear in the background scenes.

   They almost never have any lines.

   _____

   _____

5. TV sitcoms include actors and actresses.

   They are recognized by television viewers around the world.

   _____

   _____

6 *Match the definitions with the jobs.*

1. a cinematographer __g__
2. a film editor _____
3. a gossip columnist _____
4. a graphic designer _____
5. a location scout _____
6. a stagehand _____
7. a stunt person _____
8. a talk show host _____

a. a journalist who specializes in reporting on the personal lives of famous people

b. someone who looks for places to shoot scenes in a film

c. someone that helps a movie director put together the best "takes"

d. a person who does dangerous scenes in a movie in place of the main actor

e. a TV personality who invites guests to come on his or her program

f. a person who moves sets and furniture for theater and film productions

g. a person who operates the main camera during shooting

h. someone that creates the design for a printed work

---

7 *Choose a job from Exercise 6 or another job you're interested in. In the first paragraph, describe the job. In the second paragraph, describe what the job involves behind the scenes. Use relative clauses in some of your descriptions.*

    If I worked in journalism, I'd like to be a foreign correspondent like Julie McCarthy. These days, foreign correspondents, who are on call 24 hours a day, often work for both a newspaper and a broadcasting company. They meet and interview famous people all over the world.

    Behind the scenes, foreign correspondents are members of news teams, which include technicians and camera operators. Together, they try to report the news as soon as it happens, and, if possible, before any competitors!

_____
_____
_____
_____
_____

8 Describe six steps in the process of renovating a restaurant.
Use the passive form of the verbs given below.

1. designer

2. builders

3. painters

4. electrician

5. delivery people

6. owner

1. First, _a renovation plan is approved._ _____ (a renovation plan / approve)
2. Next, _____ (new walls / build)
3. Then _____ (the walls / paint)
4. After that, _____ (new lighting / install)
5. Then _____ (new furniture / deliver)
6. Finally, _____ (the restaurant / reopen)

There should be a law!

1 *What should be done about each situation? Write sentences about these pictures, giving your opinion. Use the passive form with should, shouldn't, or ought to.*

1. Leaving large items on the sidewalk

2. Eating on the subway

3. Playing loud music late at night

4. Letting dogs run without leashes

1. People shouldn't be allowed to leave large items on the sidewalk. OR

   People ought to be required to take large items to designated dumps.

2. _____

   _____

3. _____

   _____

4. _____

   _____

2 *Make recommendations about the situations in these pictures. Use the passive form with* **has to, has got to, must,** *or* **mustn't.**

1. <u>A law has to be passed to prevent people from losing their homes.</u>   OR
   <u>Something must be done to repair abandoned homes.</u>

2. _____
   _____

3. _____
   _____

4. _____
   _____

3 Think of four things that you have strong opinions about. Write your opinions and explain your reasons for them. Use passive modals.

Example: In my opinion, cell phones shouldn't be allowed in class.
They distract students from the lesson.

1. I feel that _____

_____

2. I think that _____

_____

3. In my opinion, _____

_____

4. I don't think that _____

_____

4 Respond to these opinions by giving a different one of your own. Use expressions from the box.

That's interesting, but I think . . .
That's not a bad idea. On the other hand,
 I feel . . .
You may have a point. However, I think . . .
Do you? I'm not sure . . .

1. A: Everyone should be required to study Chinese.

   B: You may have a point. However, I think that English
   is more useful for traveling.

2. A: People mustn't be allowed to write unkind things about others on social networking sites.

   B: _____

   _____

3. A: Public transportation should be provided free of charge.

   B: _____

   _____

4. A: I think people ought to be required to buy hybrid cars.

   B: _____

   _____

5. A: In my opinion, all plastic containers should be banned.

   B: _____

   _____

A Skim the web posts. What is a revenge story? Why is each of these stories a revenge story?

○○○ ◀▶ ⟳ +

Do you have a revenge story? Share it!

1 Marcy: I used to have a friend who was a lot of fun. She always loved to go out to eat. There was just one small problem: Every time the server brought the check, she would say, "Uh-oh! I don't have enough money with me. Can I pay you back later?" This was OK the first and second time it happened, but these excuses happened again and again.

I finally got my revenge. The next time we went out for dinner, I said that I had forgotten my wallet. She was shocked, but she paid the check. However, she has never called me to go out again. I guess she was a moocher – a person who always tries to get someone else to pay.

2 Jonathan: My neighbors used to keep rabbits in their yard, but they treated them very badly. Rabbit pens should be cleaned regularly, but these rabbits were dirty, and the smell was really terrible. Worse, I noticed that the rabbits didn't have enough to eat or drink. When I complained to my neighbors, they said, "It's not your problem."

When I called the animal protection society, they said they would investigate. I waited a week, but nothing happened. One night, I stole the rabbits and took them home. The next day I gave them to a local pet store.

3 Chad: I was having problems sleeping because of a dripping noise coming from my air conditioner. I thought the air conditioner needed to be repaired, so I called a technician. She couldn't find anything wrong with it, but she said the dripping was coming from the apartment above me. I asked my neighbor to have his air conditioner checked, but he said, "If you can't sleep, that's your problem!"

The following day, I climbed a ladder and attached a rubber pipe to my neighbor's air conditioner. Then I stuck the pipe through his bedroom window. The next night, my neighbor's bedroom was flooded!

B Read the posts. Then complete the chart.

Problem	First attempt to solve it	Final solution
1.		
2.		
3.		

C Do you think getting revenge – doing something mean to someone in return – is acceptable behavior? Why or why not?

6 *Add tag questions to these statements.*

1. Bullying is a serious problem, _____isn't it_____?

2. The city doesn't provide enough services for elderly people, _____does it_____?

3. You can easily spend all your money on food and rent, _____?

4. Some unemployed people don't really want to work, _____?

5. Health care is getting more and more expensive, _____?

6. There are a lot of homeless people downtown, _____?

7. Some schools have overcrowded classrooms, _____?

8. Laws should be passed to reduce street crime, _____?

7 *Nouns and verbs*

A Complete the chart.

Noun	Verb	Noun	Verb
advertisement	advertise	permission	_____
_____	bully	_____	pollute
_____	improve	prohibition	_____
offense	_____	provision	_____
_____	outsource	_____	require

B Write eight sentences with tag questions using words from the chart. Use four of the nouns and four of the verbs.

Examples: Bicyclists should be required to wear
helmets, shouldn't they?

1. _____

   _____

2. _____

   _____

3. _____

4. _____

5. _____

6. _____

7. _____

8. _____

8 **Give one reason for and one reason against these opinions.**

1. Children should be made to study a foreign language in primary school.

   For: _It would help children understand other cultures._

   Against: _I don't think it would be easy to find enough teachers._

2. Jobs shouldn't be outsourced to other countries.

   For: _____

   Against: _____

3. More tax money ought to be spent on cleaning graffiti off city walls.

   For: _____

   Against: _____

4. Stray animals should be cared for in animal centers.

   For: _____

   Against: _____

9 **Complete the conversation. Use passive modals and tag questions.**

Kate: You know, I just moved into this new apartment building, and I thought everything would be really great now.

Tony: What's the problem?

Kate: Well, yesterday, the manager gave me a copy of the house rules. I found out that I can't park my moped on the sidewalk in front of the building anymore.

Tony: But people shouldn't _____ (permit) to park their bikes or mopeds there.

Kate: Why not? There isn't any other place to park, _____ ? I guess I'll have to park on the street now.

Tony: I'm sorry that parking somewhere else will be inconvenient, but don't you agree that people shouldn't _____ (allow) to block the sidewalk or the entrance to the building?

Kate: Well, you may have a point, but parking spaces for all types of cycles need _____ (provide) for renters here. All renters with a car have a parking space, _____ ?

Tony: Well, yes, you're right. You should go to the next renter's meeting and discuss the issue with everyone else.

Kate: That's not a bad idea. My voice ought _____ (hear) as much as anyone else's – I think I will!

Challenges and accomplishments

1 *Complete the sentences with your own ideas about the jobs in the box.*

- ☐ acting in movies
- ☐ being a parent
- ☐ being a student
- ☐ being unemployed
- ☐ doing volunteer work
- ☑ teaching young children

1. One of the most rewarding aspects _of teaching young children is seeing them develop._
2. The most challenging thing _____
3. One of the rewards _____
4. One of the most difficult things _____
5. The most interesting aspect _____
6. One of the least interesting aspects _____

2 *The best and worst of it*

A Complete the chart with your own ideas.

Job	One of the best things	One of the worst things
1. social worker	helping people	
2. university professor		grading papers
3. small-business owner	making your own schedule	
4. emergency-room nurse		working long hours

B Write about the positive and negative aspects of the jobs in part A.

1. _One of the best things about being a social worker is helping people._
   One of the worst things is _____

2. _____
   _____

3. _____
   _____

4. _____
   _____

3 *Write two paragraphs about a job you find interesting. In the first paragraph, describe some positive aspects of the job. In the second paragraph, describe some of its negative aspects.*

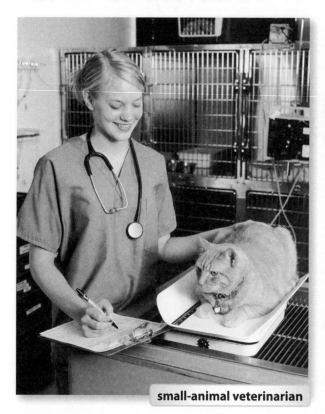
small-animal veterinarian

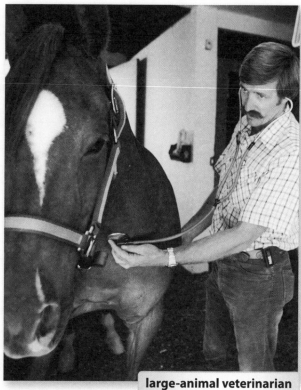
large-animal veterinarian

Being a veterinarian is both rewarding and challenging. People bring animals with different sorts of problems into the clinic every day. One of the best things about the job is treating and curing those animals that are seriously sick or injured. It's an amazing thing to be able to save an animal and bring a smile to a pet owner's face.

Sometimes, if an animal is very sick or badly injured, it's not possible to treat it successfully. The saddest aspect of the job is dealing with animals you cannot save. It's a terrible loss for both the vet and the pet owner.

_____

_____

_____

_____

_____

_____

_____

4 *Huge challenges, enormous rewards*

A Scan the first paragraph of the article. What award did *Médecins Sans Frontières* receive? When and why did they receive it?

Médecins Sans Frontières

Médecins Sans Frontières (MSF), which means "Doctors Without Borders," was established in 1971. It is now one of the world's largest organizations that provide emergency medical relief. In 1999, it won the Nobel Peace Prize. Its aim is to help people who have suffered badly in wars or natural disasters, such as earthquakes or floods.

Each year, about 3,000 people are sent abroad to work in more than 60 different countries worldwide. MSF relies on volunteer professionals but also works closely with about 25,000 locally hired staff. In most projects, there are about seven local members to every one foreigner. Volunteers are paid about $1,400 each month and receive travel expenses. They usually work on a project for six months to a year. Many volunteers go on more than one mission.

One volunteer reports, "Working in politically sensitive areas with limited resources can be frustrating, but there is huge satisfaction in making even a small or temporary difference to people. What better recommendation than to say, 'I'm about to leave on a third mission!'"

What qualities and skills do you need to become a volunteer? You have to be able to deal with stress, and you need to be able to work independently as well as in a team. You are not required to have medical qualifications. Besides medical expertise, MSF needs the skills of technical staff such as building engineers and food experts.

The reaction of volunteers returning from MSF speaks for itself. "One of my biggest challenges was organizing a team to open a new hospital in a town that had had no medical care for three years," one volunteer said. This volunteer said the project was a success because of the reduction of deaths and the fact that the local people were so thankful. Another volunteer says, "With MSF, I have had the chance to travel and test my skills to the limits both professionally and personally. The rewards can be enormous."

B Read the article. What are two challenges and two rewards of volunteering?

Challenges: _____   _____

Rewards: _____   _____

C Answer the questions.

1. What is the aim of *Médecins Sans Frontières*?

_____

2. How many countries receive foreign volunteers through MSF?

_____

3. What is the average ratio of local staff members to foreign volunteers?

_____

4. What personal qualities must volunteers have?

_____

5. What kinds of experts does MSF require?

_____

5 Choose the correct word.

1. It's not good to be _____ if you're an emergency-room nurse.
   (courageous / rigid / upbeat)

2. If teachers are going to be successful, they have to be _____ .
   (dependent / timid / resourceful)

3. You have to be _____ if you work as a volunteer.
   (adaptable / cynical / unimaginative)

4. If you take a job far from your family and friends, you have to be _____ .
   (compassionate / dependent / self-sufficient)

5. One of the most important things about working with children is being positive and not _____ .
   (adaptable / cynical / resourceful)

6. Being a role model for troubled youths requires someone who is strong and _____ .
   (compassionate / insensitive / timid)

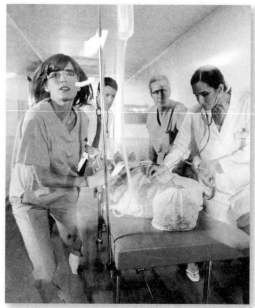

6 Choose the correct prepositions.

☑ about ☐ by ☐ for ☐ from ☐ in ☐ of

1. One of the most exciting things ___*about*___ working abroad is learning about another culture.

2. By the time I'm 35, I'd like to have lived in a culture that's very different _____ my own.

3. For me, the most difficult aspect _____ working abroad is learning a foreign language.

4. Working _____ an organization like the Peace Corps is very rewarding.

5. I'd like to have gotten another degree _____ two years.

6. I hope I'll have gotten married _____ the time I'm 30.

working abroad

7 *Accomplishments and goals*

A Match the verbs with the nouns. Write the collocations.
(More than one answer may be possible.)

Verb	Noun	
☑ buy	☐ a change	1. <u>buy a house</u>
☐ get	☐ debts	2. _____
☐ learn	☑ a house	3. _____
☐ make	☐ a promotion	4. _____
☐ meet	☐ new skills	5. _____
☐ pay off	☐ someone special	6. _____

B Write one sentence about an accomplishment and another sentence
about a goal. Use the words in part A and your own ideas.

1. <u>My sister and her husband have</u>
<u>managed to save enough money</u>
<u>to buy a house. I expect to have</u>
<u>bought a house within five years.</u>

2. _____

3. _____

4. _____

5. _____

6. _____

8 *Personal portraits*

A Write three sentences about the accomplishments of someone you know very well. Use the present perfect or simple past.

Example:

By investing his money carefully, my neighbor
Paulo was able to retire at 40. Since then, he
has managed to set up an organization that
helps find jobs for people who are homeless.
In addition, he . . .

_____

_____

_____

_____

_____

B Write three sentences about things the same person would like to have achieved in ten years. Use the future perfect or *would like to have* + past participle.

Example:

Paulo would like to have started an organization
to provide scholarships for needy college
students by the time he's 50. He hopes to
travel a lot, too. In fact, he hopes he'll have
traveled all through Southeast Asia.

_____

_____

_____

_____

_____